D0585105

Butterflies

Matthew Oates

Butterflies

*Spotting and identifying
Britain's butterflies*

 National Trust

First published in the United Kingdom in 2011 by
National Trust Books
10 Southcombe Street
London W14 0RA

An imprint of Anova Books Company Ltd

ISBN 9781907892059

A CIP catalogue for this book is available from the
British Library.

20 19 18 17 16 15 14 13 12 11
10 9 8 7 6 5 4 3 2 1

Reproduction by Mission, Hong Kong
Printed by 1010 Printing Ltd, China

This book can be ordered direct from the publisher at
the website www.anovabooks.com, or try your local
bookshop. Also available at National Trust shops,
including www.nationaltrustbooks.co.uk.

CONTENTS

THE WONDER
OF BUTTERFLIES

Over the past 25 years a minor social revolution has
occurred, quietly and subtly: butterflies have become
acceptable, if not cool. No longer is butterflying the domain
of eccentric loners, and no more are people loath to admit
their interest. The reasons for this 'coming out' and its
associated acceptance are complex but interesting.
Obviously, the demise of butterfly and moth collecting,
and its replacement by photography, has consigned a difficult
area to comic history. Butterflying has moved with the times,
in terms of values and practice. It is now as popular a
hobby as it was in the heyday of collecting, back in the
1890s, only it is now carried out using harmless
photographic equipment.

A GLORIOUS HISTORY

B utterflies have been one of the most appreciated
elements of British wildlife since before the dawn of
natural history. Our fascination with them took hold as the
wonders of their metamorphosis became apparent.

The history of our engagement with butterflies in Britain is
utterly unique. It illustrates British eccentricity at its zenith,
yet at the same time the underlying emotions of scientific
wonder and deep passion shine through gloriously. That
juxtaposition is rich and heady.

Interest in British butterflies started with the restoration of the monarchy, with Charles II's stimulation of scientific endeavour. The first book dedicated to British butterflies (as opposed to general insects) was published in 1717 by James Petiver, a London apothecary, and was called *Papilionum Britanniae*. This featured 48 species, including something quite remarkable that he called Albin's Hampstead-Eye, which is actually *Junonia villida*, a common butterfly of the Far East. Perhaps it was accidentally imported on an East India Company ship, as a caterpillar that pupated on board, before emerging and escaping in London? Incredibly, the specimen still exists in the Natural History Museum.

At this time, the first lady of butterflying, and entomology, was one Eleanor Glanville, after whom the Glanville Fritillary takes its name. She discovered the butterfly in Lincolnshire, while searching for an errant son. Later, her will was successfully overturned on account of her interest in butterflies – certain proof of insanity. The story of her romantic life is told by the historical novelist Fiona Mountain, in *Lady of the Butterflies*.

THE AURELIANS

Early enthusiasts called themselves Aurelians, seemingly after *aureolus*, from the Latin for 'golden' and referring to the colour of some butterfly pupae. The Aurelian Society was certainly in existence by 1743. In March 1748 the members were meeting in central London when the building they rented caught fire, spectacularly, and they only just escaped with their lives. Their library and collections perished – a major setback.

A second Aurelian Society started up in 1762. The leading light was one Moses Harris, who in 1766 published *The Aurelian*, which featured 33 species of butterfly and some moths, in English. This became the standard work on butterflies for some time, and included some wondrous names: the Grand Surprise or Camberwell Beauty, the Marmoress or Marbled White, the Dishclout or Greasy Frittillaria (Marsh Fritillary), and the Grizzle. Best of all, the frontispiece featured Aurelians at work in a woodland glade, wielding a clap-net or batfowler – a huge hinged net, the halves of which were clapped together to envelop a specimen. How they ever caught fast-flying butterflies in such a clumsy contraption befuddles the mind. Nearly all the British species of butterflies were discovered during the 18th or early 19th centuries.

THE GREAT VICTORIAN ERA

During the Victorian period the collecting of Lepidoptera (butterflies and moths) developed into a hugely popular pastime. Near mania was stimulated by a series of technological developments, most notably the production of more manageable nets, with cane frames and muslin bags, and the development of setting boards, on which the wings were stretched out to 'set' specimens. Entomological pins and killing fluid were also invented (though many Victorians used crushed laurel leaves, as did impoverished small boys, into the late 1960s). The major breakthrough with moth collecting came in 1841, with the invention of the technique of 'sugaring' (painting sugary and often alcoholic concoctions on tree trunks, to which moths flock). In 1879 Messers Watkins and Doncaster opened a business at 36 The Strand, London, selling equipment for those interested in collecting butterflies and moths, beetles, birds' eggs and botanical specimens. The company is still trading today, though sadly not in The Strand.

So popular did butterfly and moth collecting become that during the 1850s and 1860s six journals devoted to insect collecting were published, including *The Entomologist's Weekly Intelligencer*.

THE INFLUENCE OF THE RAILWAY

Improved transport links made a huge difference, though of course much land – especially woodland – was private and patrolled by armed gamekeepers, and arrayed with mantraps. This meant that collectors flocked to places where access was allowed, and which were close to railway stations. Great Chattenden Wood, near Rochester in north Kent, was for some decades the most popular site for woodland butterflies among London collectors.

For over a century, the New Forest in Hampshire was the premier venue for collecting butterflies and moths. A direct rail link with London was established during the 1860s and, being largely Crown land, there were rights of access. The woods and heaths were incredibly rich in butterflies and moths – over 55 per cent of the butterfly and moth fauna of the British Isles has been recorded here.

BUTTERFLYING MANIA

Up to the First World War the New Forest absorbed an annual influx of several hundred collectors. Servicing this frenzy became a major local industry, providing board and lodging, eating and drinking, transport hire, specialist guides and, interestingly, dealers in live and dead specimens. At favoured hostelries, notably *The Rose and Crown* at Brockenhurst and *The Crown Hotel* at Lyndhurst, specimens were traded, often for large sums of money. The rivalry and skulduggery was staggering, and the New Forest Keepers (Crown foresters) manipulated matters well to their own financial advantage.

The naturalist writer, W. H. Hudson, provides a scathing description of collectors at Lyndhurst in his classic book *Hampshire Days*. It is the place where:

> 'London vomits out its annual crowd of collectors, who fill its numerous and ever-increasing brand new red-brick lodging houses, and who swarm through all the adjacent woods and heaths, men, women and children (hateful little prigs!) with their vasculums, beer and treacle pots, green and blue butterfly nets, killing bottles, and all the detestable paraphernalia of what they would probably call "nature study".'

These collectors were hugely opportunistic and often ruthless.

> 'In August, 1887, whilst driving in a dog-cart from Christchurch, I saw Apatura iris (Purple Emperor) flying along the hedge… I immediately gave the reins to a friend… and pursued it with the dog-cart whip, and through a piece of luck I managed to hit the under wing above the upper, and so disable it enough to capture it. It was a fine male specimen, and not in the least damaged.'

It is probably impossible for us today to imagine the abundance of butterflies in the New Forest woods of old. S. G. Castle Russell (1866–1955) describes a visit during the hot summer of 1892:

> *As I slowly walked along, butterflies alarmed by my approach arose in immense numbers to take refuge in the trees above. They were so thick that I could hardly see ahead and indeed resembled a fall of brown leaves.*

This is what we have collectively lost. The paradise that was the New Forest woods was sacrificed on the altar of progress by the 20th-century conifer revolution. Until quite recently, those radically altered woods hosted a dearth of butterflies, though mercifully a few species are now increasing in number.

THE PURSUIT OF ABERRATIONS

The more experienced collectors looked for atypically marked (or unmarked) specimens, known as aberrations or variations – such as the White Admiral with the distinctive white bands missing (*ab nigrina*) or reduced (*ab obliterae*). Aberrations are associated with large populations and hot summers. Acutely marked specimens could realise large sums of money. F. W. Frohawk (1861–1946) sold his first collection to Lord Rothschild, and purchased a sizeable house with the proceeds.

The collectors' field-craft skills and powers of observation were immense. Castle Russell could tell, at 10yd (9m), whether a male Orange Tip, in flight, possessed the small black spot in the orange forewing splash or not (*ab immaculata*). Yet he was colour blind and could not tell left from right, which meant that he was forever getting lost in the woods.

In different eras, small swarms of collectors haunted different collecting grounds, renowned for producing aberrations. Great Chattenden Wood and the New Forest woods were the first of these, but the downs around Folkestone, Worth Matravers in Dorset and Royston in Hertfordshire were also famous, at least for certain periods.

Despite two world wars, butterfly collecting persisted as a popular pastime well into the 1960s, with many people developing the interest at school. All the time, though, quality collecting grounds were getting fewer and fewer as butterfly populations dwindled. The glory days were over. The swansong of collecting was the long hot summer of 1976.

EXTREME BUTTERFLY COLLECTING

It had not all been easy pickings. Collecting Large Heath butterflies on, or rather in, peat bogs, and swallowtails in the boggy wastes of the fens in Cambridgeshire, was decidedly risky business. As far as we know, no collector perished in the pursuit, though many returned to their lodgings thoroughly soaked, muddied and late.

The supreme tale here lies in the diaries of I. R. P. Heslop (1904–70), the last of the great British butterfly collectors, and concerns an expedition to Woodwalton Fen in July 1968. His diary recounts that when he arrived:

12

'the fen was heavily flooded… Nonetheless, I walked down to the gates, and then waded along the main drove. I was soon waist deep and then up to my armpits; and for one moment I went right under. However, I gradually found the water becoming less deep and eventually made my way through to my secret location, which was beyond the actual Reserve. Here there was only about a foot of water, and I found the Large Copper numerous.'

He took a fine series of photographs, then waded and swam back – aged 64. The diary concludes: 'I partially dried myself in the sun… and caught the 6.13 train.'

A LASTING INFLUENCE

Sydney Castle Russell, quoted on page 11, inspired a generation or two of schoolboys. For many years he called in at schools while on his collecting travels, to encourage young protégés. He developed the interest of a boy called Jones, who went on to become a house master at Christ's Hospital, the Bluecoat school in the Sussex Weald. For decades Jonah, as he was indifferently known, attempted to teach maths to disinterested juniors. On Tuesday afternoons in the summer term he did something arguably less futile: it was hobbies day and he ran a butterfly- and moth-collecting group, in that entomologically rich part of the country. He retired in the late 1960s, and his like has never been replaced. I owe that man everything, for I am the last of Jonah's boys.

THE BUTTERFLYING
EXPERIENCE TODAY

An interest in British butterflies will take you into the heart
of many of the most wonderful landscapes in our isles, at the
best time of year for them. This maximisation of place and
season is central to the very essence of the butterflying
experience. Nearly all our renowned butterfly localities
have immensely strong spirit of place.

RAISING AWARENESS

The dynamic charity Butterfly Conservation has
successfully placed butterflies and moths firmly within
the public consciousness, particularly by releasing clear
factual information to the media, in plain English. The
sad and horrific decline of these beautiful and wonderful
creatures has struck a chord within our social conscience.

On a larger scale, the UK nature conservation movement
in general has reached out to people of diverse disposition,
and has influenced the government into genuinely embracing
environmental issues. Nature conservation, including
butterflies, now features strongly within government
targets. Most notably, Butterfly Conservation has persuaded
the government to adopt butterflies as official indicators of
the general health of our environment, alongside the likes
of farmland birds.

Television has taken wildlife into people's sitting rooms,
bringing quality experiences to audiences way beyond
the reach of the nature conservation organisations.

Then there are butterfly houses – visitor centres with
butterflies flying free under cover – which have given
people direct experience and, above all, removed unnecessary
inhibitions. They have won over, or at least neutralised, many
people not normally inclined towards wildlife. Of course, true
butterfly enthusiasts tend only to visit these houses in the
depth of winter, when withdrawal symptoms are starting
to kick in.

THE LEGACY OF BIRDING

The ornithologists – the humble bird twitchers –
have done more than any other group to break down
unnecessary inhibitions and barriers to wildlife spotting,
if only by persistence and sheer numbers. This distinctive yet
varied group, in terms of social background and age, is quite
capable of descending en masse to a supermarket car park on
a Saturday morning, to view a rose-coloured starling or a flock
of waxwings, have a cup of tea in the restaurant, and join
shoppers in the aisles. In several parts of the country they
make significant contributions to the local economy, notably
in the Scilly Isles and along the north Norfolk coast and,
nationwide, anywhere that is close to RSPB and Wildfowl
and Wetland Trust nature reserves.

Butterfly people are little different, especially as they are
now bereft of nets and collecting paraphernalia, and are
bedecked instead with binoculars and cameras. The latter
distinguishes them from birders, alongside the absence of
telescopes. They too make useful contributions to local
economies, as is the case in the Norfolk Broads during June
when the Swallowtail is on the wing; on the Isle of Wight

when the Glanville Fritillaries are flying; around Bentley Wood near Salisbury, which must be the best locality for woodland butterflies today; and for villages in the Arnside and Silverdale district south of the Lake District, a major butterfly hot spot.

JOURNEYS THROUGH TIME AND PLACE

Butterflies seldom, if ever, take us into desolate environments. Although the Large Heath butterfly leads us into peat bogs, it flies when bleakness has temporarily deserted those places and the habitats are at their very best. The worst of today's experiences are urban brown-field sites or young conifer plantations harbouring spring fritillaries. Our top butterfly sites are staggeringly lovely places and surprisingly few of them suffer from traffic-noise pollution.

Those of us who consciously or subconsciously seek escapism will automatically be attracted to butterflies. Forget the mortgage and the bank statement for a few hours and get involved with butterflies instead. Best of all, no two day's butterflying are ever alike: each day, each venture is intrinsically unique, and not simply because the butterfly season changes daily. No two butterfly seasons are alike. Butterflying continuously reinvents itself.

Be warned, though, for the pursuit of butterflies can be highly addictive – it is deep magic from beyond the dawn of modern human experience. This is far more than the simple relief of stress and release of serotonin, the happiness chemical. We all need a conduit into nature, we need our hand holding; butterflying can fulfil that need.

WHAT IS A BUTTERFLY?

This question may appear facile but is actually far
from simple. It consists of many interrelated questions,
the answers to which are only partly known. Butterflies are
incredibly complex beings, and not merely on account of the
wondrous transformation that is metamorphosis. Although
they form one of the best-studied elements of British natural
history, there is still a massive amount of work to do.
The more we learn about butterflies, the more we realise
needs to be learnt. It would therefore be wise to treat
many of the following 'facts' with a little caution,
for they may change, not least with alterations
to the climate and environment.

I n simple biological terms, the butterfly is the mature
reproductive stage of a four-stage metamorphosis: egg,
caterpillar (or larva), chrysalis and finally adult butterfly.

The average lifespan of a typical small male butterfly is about
four or five days, with the females living a little longer. Some
individuals of both sexes live much longer, with those of very
small species such as Duke of Burgundy capable of living for
over three weeks. Larger butterflies may live for 10–12 days
on average. We know this from mark and recapture studies,
in which butterflies within a colony are caught, marked with
fast-drying oil-based felt-tip pens on the wing undersides,
released and recaptured. This makes it possible to determine
how long individual butterflies live, and estimate population
size and dispersal rates. The work is great fun and hugely
illuminating, helping us understand how butterflies really live.
Done properly, the butterflies are not compromised at all.

Five of our resident species overwinter as butterflies before breeding in the spring. Individuals of these species can live for eight to perhaps even 11 months. It is not unusual to see pale and ragged Brimstone butterflies that emerged the previous July or August still flying the following June; and individuals of the previous autumn's Comma brood sometimes overlap with the following midsummer's brood (their offspring).

The weather during the flight season (see below) is crucial, for a high percentage of the total brood – or locally even the entire annual brood – can be killed off by bad weather. Most butterflies can easily survive two or three poor days, but a severe deluge such as the great flood of July 2007 can be devastating, and prolonged adverse weather is equally bad. Buffeting by wind is especially damaging to them, or rain accompanied by wind.

FLIGHT SEASONS

The period during which a brood of a butterfly is on the wing is called the flight season. Although individual butterflies are often short-lived, the average flight season lasts for about five weeks. This is because individual butterflies emerge over a period of two to three weeks, often in pulses during spells of good weather.

Butterflies emerge earlier than normal during good summers and later during poor years. Seasons are so variable that normality scarcely exists. Species that are on the wing for only three to four weeks, or even less, are easily missed.

Butterfly flight seasons tend to begin with a few males, perhaps because males need to be two or three days old before they are capable of mating. A few days into the flight season there is the first of the mass emergences, consisting of many males and some females. The important peak-season period, when the butterfly is at its most numerous, is normally reached some 7–10 days after the start and lasts for a similar period, but much depends on the weather. Females dominate the later pulses of emergence, but numbers of both sexes then decline and the flight season has a lengthy tail, where just a few specimens remain.

BROODS

Many of our resident species are single-brooded, but some produce more than one brood per year. The complication here is that a species such as the Common Blue may be single-brooded in the north but double-brooded in the south. In the south, the Speckled Wood is almost continuously brooded, flying from late March through to late October.

COURTSHIP AND MATING

A biology teacher could enliven lessons by saying that being a butterfly is all about sex. It is not strictly true, although the males are certainly preoccupied with finding mates. The females, however, once mated, pursue the all-important business of laying eggs and tend to actively avoid the males like the plague.

The males of different species have different strategies for finding mates. Some are territorial, intercepting any winged intruder on the off-chance of it being a female. Many of these adopt vantage-point perches from which to strike, such as the Comma, Duke of Burgundy and Green Hairstreak.

In some species, the males search frenetically for virgin females, concentrating on major breeding grounds. Each morning Chalkhill Blue males ceaselessly patrol patches of short turf where the caterpillar's food plant, horseshoe vetch, grows, in order to seize newly emerged females. In other species, males patrol up and down a stretch of sunny lane, as in the Orange Tip, or along the foot of a steep slope, as in the Clouded Yellow.

The number of times individual males can mate is largely unknown, though in some species there appear to be alpha males who mate several times, while many other individuals are fortunate to mate once. More data are needed here.

In many of our species the females tend to mate only once, soon after emergence. Virginity does not last long in female butterflies. It cannot, for that would be a biological disadvantage. If blessed with a long life induced by good weather – or if initial mating was inadequate – females may mate twice.

Mating itself typically lasts for between 45 minutes and 1½ hours. A few species seem to specialise in mating for longer. Purple Emperors, for example, tend to pair for some 3½ hours. Commas, Peacocks, Red Admirals and Small Tortoiseshells (from the aristocrats family) pair up in the evening and may then remain 'in cop' (short for *in copula*, which translates from the Latin as 'into a bond') all night.

Some butterflies have elaborate courtship flights, especially
the Grayling. A pair of Grayling will face each other on the
ground, and indulge in a lengthy session of amorous interplay
involving antennae and forelegs. White Admiral males will
follow a female for some time, mimicking her every move.
In many species, however, courtship is non-existent. To
anthropomorphise, he may not even ask the lady's name.

EGG LAYING

The technical term for the laying of eggs is oviposition. It is
thought that a female butterfly who mates in the morning may
begin to lay her eggs (oviposit) towards the end of that day,
the first of her adult life.

How many eggs a butterfly lays depends on many factors,
including the weather. Some appear to lay only a very small
number of eggs, as is the case with the Wall Brown and
Mountain Ringlet. Following the females of these two in the
hope of watching eggs being laid is incredibly unrewarding
work. Most of our butterflies are far more productive,
regularly laying single eggs. The basic pattern is to lay, fly
away, rest, feed on a flower, locate another egg-laying site,
and so on. Six of our species lay huge batches of eggs (Large
White, Glanville, Heath and Marsh Fritillaries, Peacock and
Small Tortoiseshell), which often consist of 250 eggs or more.
Some females of these appear to return to their original batch
to add more eggs, even on different days.

A female butterfly lays her eggs on the right species of plant
(the food plant), in the right situation and condition to
support the resultant larvae. Female butterflies are incredibly

pernickety about where they lay their eggs, and with good reason: they are ensuring the survival of their species.

To study a butterfly's ecology you need to know where the females lay their eggs. A few butterflies refuse to play ball here. For example, I have failed spectacularly to watch female Heath Fritillaries laying eggs on Exmoor, where their habitats are dominated by dense bracken. Also, very occasionally this technique can be misleading. The female Large Blue lays her eggs in the buds of wild thyme, on which the young larvae feed for a while. But the caterpillar of the Large Blue is primarily a carnivore, devouring the grubs of the red ant *Myrmica sabuleti*. For decades, experts were fooled into thinking that wild thyme was the food plant for the Large Blue, whereas it is only the starter course.

BREEDING GROUNDS

Many of our butterflies have discrete and localised breeding grounds, which may form only a small percentage of the flight area used by the highly mobile adults. Often, a colony (or population) is dependent on a scatter of pockets of suitable breeding areas. This is very much the case with some of the butterflies I have attempted to study, notably the Pearl-bordered and High Brown Fritillaries. Actual primary breeding areas can be tiny and a female butterfly must find these small, isolated hot spots. She faces many obstacles, including amorous males congregating in these vital areas in search of virgin females. Worse, it seems that many breeding areas oscillate in and out of suitability, especially in relation to seasonal variation in plant growth. This is a vital point in the conservation of butterflies.

The larvae of most British butterflies are restricted to feeding on a narrow range of plants, usually a small number of species from the same plant genus. These favoured plants are known among butterfly people as food plants.

Some 10 or 11 of our butterfly species feed only on a single species of plant, such as the White Admiral which breeds on honeysuckle and the Adonis Blue which breeds solely on horseshoe vetch. More often, a butterfly is strongly associated with one plant, though it will use some others in odd situations; for example, the Red Admiral breeds largely but not exclusively on common stinging nettle.

Seventeen of our resident butterflies breed on grasses, or grasses and sedges to be more precise. These vary from small fine-leaved grasses such as sheep's fescue, with which the Small Heath is associated, to tall coarse grasses like tor grass, the sole food plant of the Lulworth Skipper. Seven or so species utilise trees and shrubs. Purple Emperor, Purple Hairstreak and White-letter Hairstreak breed on trees – sallows, oaks and elms respectively.

PLANT QUALITY

The food plant must be in the right condition to feed the caterpillars, or they will perish. All too often, though, it is not – even on well-managed nature reserves. Commonly, food plants can be hidden among dense vegetation, in which case they grow in too cool and moist a microclimate, assuming the females can even find them. We are still in the process of understanding how fastidious butterflies – and especially their caterpillars – are about food-plant quality and quantity.

The matter of food plants is complicated further by the fact that several of our butterflies breed on a variety of plants that grow in different places. The most extreme example here is the Green Hairstreak, which is associated mainly with common rockrose and birdsfoot trefoil on the downs, gorse on heaths, bilberry on upland moors and cranberry in peat bogs, and overspills on to quite a few other plants as well. So this local butterfly occurs in a diversity of habitats, breeding on a wide range of plants.

THE EGG STAGE

The technical term for an egg is ovum (singular), with the plural being ova, from the Latin.

The eggs of many of our butterflies are quite easy to find, partly because eggs are more numerous than any other butterfly life stage. Many are distinctively coloured, usually in pale shades, and only a few match the leaves or stems to which they are attached. Some are surprisingly large, like those of the Large and Silver-spotted Skippers. Others are relatively smaller in comparison, like those of the Painted Lady and Red Admiral.

Nine of our resident butterflies overwinter as eggs, including four of the hairstreaks. Finding the eggs of Brown, Purple and White-letter Hairstreaks is staple winter entertainment for many butterfly enthusiasts, especially as these species are actually most readily found as winter eggs.

Mostly, the egg stage lasts between 10 and 21 days depending on the weather, with the tiny caterpillar eating its way out through a hole in the egg roof, and usually devouring much of the egg case as its first meal.

Little is known about egg mortality but egg parasites – microscopic wasp-like creatures – affect some butterflies. There are also predatory invertebrates to contend with, and the likelihood of viral infections. It is, however, much safer being an egg than a caterpillar. Tiny caterpillars desiccate badly in hot weather, and all caterpillar stages are vulnerable to predators, parasites and viruses.

THE CATERPILLAR STAGE

The correct technical term is larva, plural larvae. The caterpillars of most British butterflies are rather mundane to look at, being smooth and green and relying on camouflage. The bright, hairy caterpillars one sees nearly all belong to moths, though caterpillars from the family *Nymphalidae* (fritillaries and aristocrats) have impressive spines. The caterpillars of the Swallowtail and Purple Emperor are truly spectacular. When full grown, the former is green-grey with black stripes punctuated by orange spots, and can raise an impressive pair of horns; the latter matches the green of the sallow leaves it devours, but has some pale yellow stripes and a massive pair of horns. Both caterpillars reach the size of your little finger. The caterpillars of nearly all our butterflies spin copious amounts of silk, usually to form a pad on which to rest, digest and grow.

The vast majority of our butterflies overwinter in the caterpillar stage, mostly as very small caterpillars. Most hibernate completely, but some are active on mild winter days.

Caterpillars are most remarkable creatures and should never be underestimated. They are capable of dynamic growth, periodically changing their skins to the next size up. Some can grow from minuscule to 2cm (¾in) in length in a month, though growth is hampered by cool or wet weather. Some survive being buried in flood water, like those of the Swallowtail and Large Heath. I have known the bulk of a group of Marsh Fritillary caterpillars to extricate itself after being trampled into the mud by cattle. Marsh Fritillary caterpillars also seem to be almost fireproof, for I have known them survive Easter grass fires in healthy numbers.

CATERPILLAR PREDATORS AND PARASITES

Caterpillars are highly vulnerable to predation, particularly before their first skin change and when they are changing their skins. Birds and invertebrates are the main culprits. Two-thirds of the wild hibernating caterpillars of the Purple Emperor I studied were eaten, presumably by tits and mainly during the late winter period. Some caterpillars seem to be toxic to many predators. The Large White is a good example here.

There are numerous minute parasitic flies and wasps, the females of which 'sting' their eggs through the caterpillar's skin. The grubs of these parasites then feed inside the caterpillar as it grows, eventually emerging from the caterpillar or the chrysalis. They are clever creatures as they only kill their host late on. Little is known about them, not least because they are hard to identify. Some are rare in themselves, being restricted to one or two host species only. An extreme example here is *Neotypus melanocephalus*, a tiny wasp that parasitises caterpillars of the Large Blue deep down inside ant nests, after first fooling the worker ants by squirting something nasty at them. It is even rarer than the Large Blue itself. The more familiar Holly Blue is heavily parasitised by another little wasp, *Listrodomus nycthemerus*.

I have spent much time studying parasite levels on Marsh Fritillary caterpillars at a site in Gloucestershire. Each March I determine the number of the minute white cocoons of the minuscule parasitic wasp *Cotesia bignelli* and the number of dead and dying Marsh Fritillary caterpillars. Twelve years on it appears that the parasite is no real problem for the butterfly there.

The truth is that the caterpillars of most of our butterflies have not been studied properly in the wild. Study is not easy, as many are solitary and nocturnal. I found that those of the Duke of Burgundy became active only after 10pm, and then only when the night was dry and the temperature exceeded 10°C (50°F). The caterpillars of the Mountain Ringlet have never been found in the wild.

Victorian and, especially, Edwardian butterfly collectors were much better at finding caterpillars than today's butterfly enthusiasts. Many of their skills need rediscovering.

THE CHRYSALIS STAGE

The correct term for a chrysalis is a pupa (plural pupae). The verb for what the caterpillar does to form it is, to pupate. This stage must not be confused with cocoons, the dense silk tents within which many moths pupate. None of our butterflies pupate within proper cocoons, though several spin a few threads of silk together, or draw a leaf closed with a few strands of silk.

Ten British butterflies overwinter in the pupal state, but for most species the pupal state lasts for three to four weeks, depending on the weather. Mortality rates may well be high, due to predation, viruses and parasites, but we do not really know. For many species, it seems that the longer the pupal period is prolonged by poor weather, the higher the mortality rate will be, while hot weather brings out the butterfly in better numbers.

We do not know where most of our butterflies pupate. The pupae of many species have scarcely been found in the wild, and much is inferred from breeding in captivity. I have only found the pupae of 20 of our species in the wild; few experts will have found more. Caterpillars of many of our blue butterflies, and of the Purple Hairstreak, appear to pupate regularly in ant nests. Do not underestimate a caterpillar!

IDENTIFYING
BUTTERFLIES

Butterfly identification is a difficult but enjoyable challenge. It takes years to master and there is no fast route. Additionally, most people's eyesight deteriorates with age, which means that anyone taking up butterflying after the age of about 50 may have missed their best window of opportunity. There are butterflies a 30-year-old can identify with ease, which later become a struggle. Sadly, butterflies seem to become smaller as one ages.

I dentification skills develop gradually with experience. Experience builds confidence, which in turn breeds competence – assuming that the eyesight holds up. Close-focusing binoculars are a huge help, although it does take time to master using them on small, fast-moving and often distant objects. Experienced birders, used to focusing 'bins' on birds in flight, will quickly master nearly all our butterflies.

It would seem wise to leave the more difficult species until you have mastered the easy ones. However, some of our commonest butterflies are among the hardest to identify: separating the Large, Small and Green-veined Whites is one of the most challenging aspects of British butterfly identification. Some of the species most in need of our attention are also difficult, notably the High Brown and Dark-green Fritillaries, and the two Pearl-bordered Fritillaries.

Using a butterfly net is scarcely an option, as most butterflies are extremely hard to catch and also because of the risk of being mistaken for a butterfly collector. Rightly or wrongly, you can get lynched on a nature reserve for wielding a butterfly net these days.

COLOUR CONFUSION

The challenge is made greater by the fact that the males and females of some 20 of the 60 species seen annually in the UK are differently coloured (known as sexual dimorphism). For example, the sexes of the Common Blue and Orange Tip differ considerably. In others the differences are subtle.

The greatest area of confusion is with female blues and the Brown Argus. The female Common Blue can be blue or brown, like a Brown Argus. The females of the Chalkhill and Adonis Blues are hard to separate, especially if there are female Common Blues around – and there will be – not to mention Brown Arguses. Both sexes of the Small and Essex Skippers are almost impossible to separate unless you see them close up (or through binoculars) head on, and even then you may not always be sure, or right.

Size is not a particularly useful characteristic, as most of the confusing species are of a similar size. Moreover, size in many species is not constant; large and small specimens occur, especially among the whites and the blues.

Even worse, the colours on butterfly wings are formed from myriad delicate scales that rub off as the butterfly ages, or in adverse weather. The wings also tear, notably on brambles. So, an old individual can look radically different from fresher specimens, and can be extremely hard to identify.

Some butterfly species flop around in loose colonies in flowery grassland, sipping nectar and displaying their wings obligingly to the hapless beginner. They are the easy ones.

Those situations are not that common. More often, butterfly spotting consists of searching hard for a handful of small, fast-flying butterflies in dense bushes on difficult terrain, or lost among clouds of common butterflies. All too often success consists of momentary sightings – the moment when one of the black specks intermittently flitting about high on an ash tree descends, does a quick twirl, half-revealing itself as a probable Black Hairstreak before ascending again to the tree tops. That would be quite a reasonable sighting of that elusive species, and may be it for the day.

HALLUCINATIONS AND PERMUTATIONS

Frequent tricks of light mean you will hallucinate butterflies, especially Purple Emperors. You will see things when you least expect them. Be careful, for some of those visions will be real.

You must learn to identify all the different permutations of each species of butterfly: flying in dull weather and bright sun; near and far; high and low; into and with the sun; full frontal and obscured by leaves; wings open and wings closed; floating in calm weather or buffeted and carried by the wind; pristine freshly emerged specimens and faded antiquities. Many species behave differently in different situations. The situations of experience are infinite, and you need to master them all.

Welcome to the world of butterflying. If you like the thrill of the chase, new learning experiences, and the pursuit of beauty and rarity, this is the hobby for you. The essential requirements are quite simple: constant vigilance and permanent concentration, nothing less. Never relax – you might miss out on a unique experience.

BASIC PRINCIPLES

There are some principles that will help the beginner enormously. In particular, a sound knowledge of butterfly habitats and flight seasons will assist identification greatly.

HABITAT

A habitat is a place that holds all the things a butterfly requires, notably the food plant of its caterpillar. Many butterflies, including most of our scarcer species, only breed in, and seldom stray from, specific habitats. So, learn the butterfly habitats assiduously, and how to identify butterfly food plants. You will not see a Large Heath on a sand dune, but you may well see a large female Small Heath there. Also, you are most unlikely to see an Adonis Blue unless its sole food plant, horseshoe vetch, is present. This plant is easy to spot in early summer when it is in flower, and the Adonis first brood is on the wing, but is hard to pick out later in the summer, when the Adonis' second brood is flying. There is no excuse for confusing Glanville and Heath Fritillaries in the UK, as they have never occurred in the same localities, while the similar-looking Mountain Ringlet and Scotch Argus fly at different times of year in different places.

The timing of the flight seasons of most of our butterflies is reasonably precise. But they do vary from year to year: there are early and late years, corresponding to good and poor summers. Also, confusingly, there is much regional variation, with a species flying two to three weeks earlier in the warm south than in the cooler north. There are even 'early' and 'late' sites within a county or district, with 'early' sites occurring on hot south-facing slopes and 'late' sites on cool north-facing slopes or in damp woods. This local asymmetry is probably most acute in the Chalkhill Blue. The largest colonies tend to produce both early and late individuals.

Climate change seems to be making these flight seasons occur earlier and earlier, which may allow some species to fit in extra broods. You will need to keep up to speed with these developments, which is easily done by becoming an active member of Butterfly Conservation.

UPPER SIDES AND UNDERSIDES

Ten British butterflies settle only with their wings closed, which means that you need to become familiar with their undersides. These are the Grayling, Small Heath, Large Heath, Green Hairstreak, Black Hairstreak, White-letter Hairstreak, Clouded Yellow, Brimstone and the two Wood Whites.

MALE V. FEMALE

Finally, much of the time there are significant differences between male and female behaviour. The males tend to be

33

more active and are often more colourful, which means you tend to notice them more than the females, even though the actual sex ratio may be fairly even. The males of many species are territorial and aggressive. This means that the butterfly you thought was a female Common Blue seen defending a territory against all-comers was actually a male Brown Argus. There is no excuse for mistaking a male Brown Argus – the belligerence is blatant.

TIPS FOR BEGINNERS

- Master the easy species first and leave the difficult ones till later. Feel unabashed at lumping Small and Essex Skippers together, and treating the Large and Small Whites as 'cabbage whites' – instead enjoy your easy Marbled Whites and Peacocks.
- Concentrate on the brighter, showier and more prominent males. It is wise to ignore the female blues at first, for example, and get to know them through observing the mating pairs.
- Learn the habitats, food plants and flight seasons. They will provide general guidance.
- Use binoculars. It also makes people think you are a birder, and not a weirdo.
- Seek help. Join a local wildlife group and attend some field meetings.

BUTTERFLY PHOTOGRAPHY

Photographing butterflies in the wild has recently developed into a popular and deeply satisfying hobby. It is a positive use of the hunting gene in us, providing a thrill-of-the-chase experience and leaving us with something beautiful to keep or share. There is considerable scope for individual photographic style. Most participants seek to obtain perfect photographs of pristine specimens of all our indigenous butterflies in their natural settings. Some, though, specialise in the butterflies of individual regions, counties or habitats, and all butterfly photographers have their favourite species, habitats and seasons.

At present, still-camera technology only enables most photographers to target perched butterflies, but sooner or later it will enable people to photograph butterflies properly in flight. The hobby is poised to enter new dimensions, borne on the wings of rapid technological development.

EQUIPMENT

This is not, of course, an inexpensive hobby, though much can be achieved with fairly basic equipment. It is vital to have the best camera and lens you can afford. Nearly all keen butterfly photographers today use digital SLR cameras with large megapixel capacity, though many compact cameras are surprisingly good. Until recently many practitioners used flash, largely for infill, though too much flash will bring out colours on a butterfly's wing that are not normally seen, and spoil the image.

Photographers spend much time, often on winter evenings, putting the summer's pictures through Photoshop software to correct or improve them further. There are some seriously good and relatively cheap software packages available, which enable you to sharpen a fuzzy image, alter the colours and remove interfering objects, such as intrusive grass stems, by cloning and infilling with more appropriate material. Photoshop can also largely sort out the common problems of over- and under-exposure, and add infill flash.

Not only is the camera important, but also the printer, and its ink and paper, and it is wise to calibrate your computer screen and printer to the same colour range. Hardened butterfly photographers probably spend as much time processing their images as taking them.

SOME PHOTOGRAPHIC CHALLENGES

Obviously, butterflies are small moving objects, and most of them are frightful fidgets. Camera (or film) speed is a major issue, with a shutter speed of at least 125 being necessary. Depth of field is also critical: use a minimum aperture setting of F8, not least because butterflies often sit with their wings held in a V-shape. In this situation, it is best to photograph a butterfly from the side, rather than from above, to ensure that most or all of the subject is in focus. In close-up photographs of V-perched butterflies taken from above, the body or wing tips are invariably out of focus. As a general rule, it is best to focus on the insect's head, which ensures that the antennae are properly in focus (photos of butterflies with their antennae out of focus are highly unsatisfactory, but common).

When basking, butterflies hold their wings out flat, which helps the photographer to resolve the depth-of-field issue. Avoid casting a shadow over the butterfly, which will either make it fly off or dull the colours. Butterflies settled with their wings closed are relative easy to photograph, though of course this exposes only the wing undersides, which are usually both less colourful and less interesting.

In close-up photographs of butterflies the background is often a complete blur. This can dominate an otherwise good photo, though the problem can often be reduced or solved by cropping. The photographer must decide what backgrounds to accept and reject, and assess background potential at the same time as assessing the actual butterfly. Bits of foliage often get in the way – this is particularly an issue with butterflies that settle among long grass.

PICK YOUR BUTTERFLY

Some species of butterfly are more approachable than others or, to be more accurate, some are more wary than others. Suitable butterflies for beginners are Marbled White, Ringlet, Chalkhill and Adonis Blues, and the common showy aristocrats – the Peacock and Small Tortoiseshell. Some species are very nervous and unapproachable, including some common butterflies like the Speckled Wood. Strong-flying species, such as Clouded Yellow and Dark-green Fritillary, present a serious challenge, as do the tree-top hairstreaks and Purple Emperor. A few butterflies are shutter-shy, flying off as the shutter clicks and presenting the photographer with a lovely background shot, sometimes with a blur of a butterfly taking off. The Wall Brown is the supreme champion here.

By and large, the females are more passive and more easily approached than the males, though they are often less colourfully marked. The same is true of old and tired specimens. Meanwhile, patrolling males are particularly difficult to photograph.

All too often butterflies fly off when you get close enough to shoot a photo. It is best to approach a butterfly from out of the shadows, rather than from between it and the sun. Often you need to crouch down, or crawl. Some butterflies, notably the Purple Emperor, force you to lie prostrate, much to the bemusement of other people walking by.

WEATHER CONDITIONS

If you think that hot, bright sunshine provides the best conditions for photographing butterflies, think again. In such weather butterflies can be too active to approach, or worse, they settle only with their wings closed in order to protect their bodies from overheating. Wind is the devil incarnate. Most butterflies hate it for a start, and it makes photography extremely difficult, and at times pointless.

Pale sun provides the best light for butterfly photography, particularly if light conditions are stable and are not changing constantly as small clouds pass. Calm, cloudy days with incipient brightness actually provide the best conditions, as many butterflies then bask with their wings open, trying to warm up. These are definitely the best conditions for photographing the exquisite Large Blue.

- Use a monopod. This keeps the camera steady.

- Visit butterflies that are at roost. They are far more approachable then, though sun angles can be rather difficult.

- Mating pairs tend to be somewhat preoccupied and are far more approachable than individual butterflies.

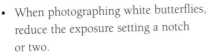

- When photographing white butterflies, reduce the exposure setting a notch or two.

- Try backlighting – photographing a perched butterfly with bright light behind it. This works especially well with species like the Brimstone and Marbled White.

- Above all, develop your own photography style. Choose the right day for photographing butterflies, pick your individual butterflies with care, and work out how to approach and, crucially, placate them. Relax and enjoy, this is a truly wonderful hobby.

- On rainy days, try photographing butterflies roosting among long grass. They look exquisite when covered in rain droplets, especially the Marbled White and the Meadow Brown.

- Spot and follow the one butterfly that is being calm and placid – usually it will have only recently emerged or just finished mating. Avoid more frenetic butterflies!

BUTTERFLY SPECIES

Most living things have both an English name and a scientific name. Our own species is man, or Homo sapiens. *A species is defined as a group of living things that produce similar-looking individuals through reproduction, and are largely incapable of interbreeding with another species (though there are exceptions). Taxonomy is the science of the classification of living (and extinct) things, which uses nomenclature, or systematic naming. Our butterflies have the most glorious names, both English and scientific, which are the legacy of centuries of wonder and study, and are an essential part of the appeal of these creatures.*

WHAT'S IN A NAME?

B utterfly names are not fixed in tablets of stone, much as they might merit it, but have always been subject to alteration, according to changes in taxonomic knowledge and fashion. Changes are regularly made to the scientific names – so much so that, at present, the English or common names tend to be more reliable.

ENGLISH OR COMMON NAMES

These attempt to be descriptive, though in a rather unique language. Skippers skip in flight, swallowtails have long forked-wing tails, hairstreaks have fine hair-like lines on the hindwing undersides, and tortoiseshells are tortoiseshell. Without doubt, the English names capture the characters we attribute to our butterflies.

It took decades for the English names of our butterflies to be agreed, as different names were ascribed by different pioneer authors. For example, the Silver-washed Fritillary was originally recorded as the Greater Silver-streaked Fritillary (in 1699); 11 years later another author named it the Silver-stroaked Fritillary; then, in 1717, the sexes, which differ visibly, were named the Greater Silverstreakt Orange Fritillary (males) and the Greater Silverstreakt Golden Fritillary (females). In a book of 1769 the insect was recognised as a single species, called the Great Fritillary. The Victorians finally determined it as the Silver-washed Fritillary. They settled matters – now it is known only as the Silver-washed Fritillary. Since the late Victorian era, English names have remained relatively constant.

MOTH NAMES

If anything, the common names of moths are even more captivating. Many of the family names are wonderful: there are families of footman moths, hawkmoths, hooktips, pugs, underwings and wainscots. Many of the individual species names are remarkable – the Death's Head Hawkmoth is unforgettable. Other wondrous names include the Alchymist, Brussels Lace, Chimney Sweeper, Double Kidney, Emperor Moth and Feathered Gothic. Merveille du Jour and True Lover's Knot are also impressive, but the pick of the bunch has to be the Setaceous Hebrew Character, a thoroughly boring common grey moth that irritates moth enthusiasts by being annoyingly abundant in moth traps.

Traditionally, our butterflies have belonged to seven major families, though two of these have only single British representatives. These families are the skippers (*Hesperiidae*), swallowtails (*Papilionidae*), whites and yellows (*Pieridae*), blues, coppers and hairstreaks (*Lycaenidae*), metalmarks (*Riodinidae*), fritillaries and aristocrats (*Nymphalidae*) and the browns (*Satyridae*). Recently, however, the *Satyridae* has been sunk within the *Nymphalidae*, which means that at present there are only these six families worldwide. For some reason the families run in the order given above.

THE MYSTERIES OF SCIENTIFIC NAMES

Species names are mainly Greek or Latin and normally consist of two words. The first identifies the genus (like a surname, within which all the individual species have characteristics in common). The genus or generic name always begins with a capital letter. The second name is the specific name of the individual species within that genus (the equivalent of a first name) and is written entirely in the lower case. Scientific names are usually given in italics, or are underlined, or appear in brackets.

As an example, the Purple Emperor bears the scientific name *Apatura iris*, *Apatura* being the genus and *iris* the specific name. Ah, but what do those words mean? Well, *Apatura* is probably derived from a Greek verb meaning 'to deceive', though it also alludes to the Athenian festival of the Apaturia, which celebrated the goddess Athena. Iris was the winged messenger of the gods, who appeared to mortal man in the guise of a rainbow. Both words reflect aspects of the shimmering iridescent colours of the male Purple Emperor. In text, scientific names can be shortened after the first full mention, so that *Apatura iris* becomes simply *A. iris* in subsequent mentions.

DIRECTORY OF BUTTERFLY SPECIES

THE SKIPPERS (*Hesperiidae* family)

Skippers are small, fast-moving butterflies. Most are orange or bright brown and are creatures of flowery grassland.

CHEQUERED SKIPPER (*Carterocephalus palaemon*)

This skipper lives only in the western Highlands of Scotland, flying from mid-May to mid-June – seeing it is one of the best butterflying experiences. It inhabits damp grassy places among bracken or open woodland, favouring sheltered hollows. It loves bugle flowers and breeds on coarse grasses, especially purple moor grass. *Carterocephalus* means strong-headed.

DESCRIPTION: A small black-and-yellow skipper that flies low and often fast, regularly disappearing. It can only be confused with the Duke of Burgundy, which does not occur in Scotland.

SMALL SKIPPER AND ESSEX SKIPPER
(*Thymelicus sylvestris* and *T. lineola*)

Two near-identical skippers that fly together in rough grassland. The Small Skipper starts to emerge 10 days or so before the Essex, flying from late June to late August and overlapping with the Essex. Both occur in colonies in similar rough grassland habitats and behave similarly, but they breed on different coarse grasses and Essex Skipper prefers disturbed ground. The Small Skipper is confined mainly to places where Yorkshire fog grass grows. *Sylvestris* means 'of the wood', which is odd as the Small Skipper is a grassland insect; *lineola* (Essex Skipper) refers to the small line on the upper side of the male's forewing.

DESCRIPTION: Both are bright orange skippers (see colour section). Look head-on at the undersides of the antennae of a specimen at rest or visiting a tall flower: if the undersides are dipped in jet-black ink, it is an Essex Skipper. Be careful, as female Small Skippers often have antennae that have dark brown undersides. If in any doubt, record it as Small/Essex Skipper or *Thymelicus* sp.

LULWORTH SKIPPER (*Thymelicus acteon*)

A tiny skipper that occurs only in Dorset, and then just on limestone soils where rough tor grass, its sole food plant, grows. Flies from late June to late August, but there are 'early' and 'late' localities. It loves flowers such as marjoram, scabious and knapweeds, and is plentiful where it occurs. Named after Actaeon, a character from Greek mythology who, while hunting, voyeuristically watched the goddess Artemis bathing and was punished by being turned into a stage and promptly chased and eaten by his own hounds.

DESCRIPTION: It can look quite dark (males) or light, like a diminutive Small Skipper (females). Females have a pale orange flared circle on the forewing upper side. Its small size separates it from the Small Skipper.

SILVER-SPOTTED SKIPPER (*Hesperia comma*)

This lovely skipper flies from late July to early September, but occurs only on very short chalk grassland turf in central southern and south east England. It is easy to identify as the similar-looking Large Skipper does not skim short turf and is nearly finished for the year by the time the Silver-spotted Skipper emerges. Breeds on semi-isolated tussocks of sheep's fescue grass in short downland turf.

DESCRIPTION: The silver spots on the hindwing undersides are distinctive. It flies fast and very low, and is hard to follow.

LARGE SKIPPER (*Ochlodes sylvanus*)

A common butterfly that flies from early June to mid-August. Colonies occur anywhere in England and Wales with rough grasses, on which the larvae feed. This is a bold, harrier jump jet in character. When settled it often holds its hindwings horizontally flat while the forewings are held at an angle of 45 degrees.

DESCRIPTION: Prominent orange-and-black markings (see colour section). An amazingly fast-flying butterfly – males chase each other about at high speed.

GRIZZLED SKIPPER (*Pyrgus malvae*)

Seen from late April to mid-June, on dry grasslands and in woodland clearings, this butterfly tends to bask with wings open on bare ground. It breeds mainly on wild strawberry and common tormentil.

DESCRIPTION: This grey-and-white chequered butterfly is tiny, fast-flying and easily lost. It is difficult to follow in bright sunlight. Not readily confused with any other butterfly or small moth.

DINGY SKIPPER (*Erynnis tages*)

Flies from late April to mid-June, with the odd second brood specimen appearing during August in hot summers. An insect of short grassland, especially downland, breeding on birdsfoot trefoil and horseshoe vetch. The males are belligerent, fighting with other male butterflies. The Dingy Skipper aptly belongs to the genus *Erynnis*, derived from the Erynyes or Greek Furies, a gang of nasty, snake-haired winged creatures that harried wrongdoers.

DESCRIPTION: You may mistake this dull brown butterfly for a moth, only it is a superbly strong and agile flier, and settles with open wings. No moth is such a masterly flier. See also the Burnet Companion moth (page 74), which has similar forewings but orange hindwings.

THE SWALLOWTAILS (*Papilionidae* family)

Only one species of the large family of worldwide swallowtails
occurs in the UK – a shame, as they are the most spectacular
of all the butterflies.

SWALLOWTAIL (*Papilio machaon*)

Now found only in the main river valleys of the Norfolk
Broads, where it is seldom numerous, it breeds on milk
parsley, a scarce wetland plant. In calm, sunny weather the
butterflies freely visit flowers, notably marsh thistles, ragged
robin and flag iris. They retreat to the reed beds in windy
weather, even if it is sunny. Swallowtails fly during June but a
small second brood occurs during August in warm summers.
Migratory individuals of the continental subspecies, *gorganus*,
occasionally stray into our southern counties. If our climate
warms up they may well colonise, as *gorganus* breeds on
several relatively common plants, including wild carrot. The
UK species is named after Machaon, a Greek doctor in the
Trojan wars.

DESCRIPTION: There is no mistaking this giant butterfly, our
largest. It can be spotted in flight at 200m (220yd), appearing
coffee-coloured. Most sightings of it are distant and brief. It is
best seen from a boat on the Norfolk Broads, patrolling over
the reed beds.

THE WHITES AND YELLOWS
(*Pieridae* family)

This butterfly family consists of the cabbage whites and other white butterflies, the distinctive Orange Tip, the yellow Brimstone and the golden Clouded Yellow.

THE WOOD WHITES (*Leptidea sinapis, L. reali*)

Real's Wood White is currently known only from Ireland, whereas the true Wood White occurs patchily in southern England, where it is in rapid decline. Both breed on greater birdsfoot trefoil, and the Wood White also uses other members of the pea family, notably yellow meadow vetchling and bitter vetch. The Wood White is wrongly named *sinapis* after the mustard plant, with which it has no association. It flies in narrow woodland rides and other sheltered grassland habitats, but also on the scrubby cliffs of the south-east Devon coast. Real's Wood White seems to occur in more open habitats, including sand dunes. They fly mainly during late May and June, with a second brood occurring in Wood White populations in the far south during late July and early August.

DESCRIPTION: Settle only with closed wings. The two species can be separated only by examining the male genitalia, Real's having a long penis – but do not try identifying it this way.

THE CLOUDED YELLOWS
(*Colias croceus, C. hyale* and *C. alfacariensis*)

The Clouded Yellow is unmistakeable. Two other species (Pale and New Pale Clouded Yellow) can occur in the British Isles,

Red Admiral
(*Vanessa atalanta*)

Silver-washed Fritillary
(*Argynnis paphia*)

Green-veined White
(*Pieris napi*)

Orange Tip
(*Anthocharis cardamines*)

Chalkhill Blue
(*Polyommatus coridon*)

Large Skipper
(*Ochlodes sylvanus*)

Peacock
(*Aglais io*)

Small Copper
(*Lycaena phlaeas*)

Small Skipper (*Thymelicus sylvestris*) and Essex Skipper (*T. lineola*)

Large White (*Pieris brassicae*)
and Small White (*P. rapae*)

Holly Blue
(*Celastrina argiolus*)

Gatekeeper
(*Pyronia tithonus*)

but your chances of seeing these are excessively slim. Clouded Yellows are swift-flying migrant butterflies that come from the Mediterranean or beyond, mainly in hot summers. The males patrol the bottoms of south-facing slopes, pausing to visit flowers or settle on bare ground. The females lay eggs on stunted vetches and clovers growing in hot, bare ground situations. The butterflies are seen mainly during August and September, often resultant from June immigrants.

Look out for fields of clover or, better still, lucerne during a Clouded Yellow immigration year. Red clover is often grown on organic farms today, and is usually allowed to flower, attracting Clouded Yellows from far and wide, though they are invariably male. You will not forget a good Clouded Yellow summer. Do not miss out.

DESCRIPTION: Settle only with closed wings. The Clouded Yellow is our only gold-and-black butterfly and is unmistakeable – *croceus* means saffron-coloured – though a few of the females are white and black (called form *helice*).

BRIMSTONE (*Gonepteryx rhamni*)

This large and distinctive butterfly can be seen at almost any time of year. It is long-lived, emerging mainly in July and over-wintering before reappearing to pair up and lay eggs in spring. It breeds on buckthorn bushes, which occur locally over much of lowland England and Wales. A loner and a great wanderer that gets almost everywhere.

DESCRIPTION: Settles only with closed wings. The males are distinctive, almost golden in bright sunshine, but the pale greenish-white females are less evident (see colour section).

LARGE WHITE AND SMALL WHITE
(*Pieris brassicae* and *P. rapae*)

Size normally differentiates the two ubiquitous cabbage whites, but dwarf Large Whites readily occur. Both species are found in all lowland places from April through to autumn, and are commonest during August. They breed on various wild and cultivated members of the cabbage family, *Cruciferae*. Learn to tell the two apart by watching them together on a garden buddleia.

DESCRIPTION: Large Whites tend to have larger and darker black markings on the forewing tips, especially the females (see colour section).

GREEN-VEINED WHITE (*Pieris napi*)

Flies in two main broods, in spring and high summer, with a patchy local third brood emerging after hot summers. Widespread throughout the UK, breeding on various wild and garden cruciferous plants, though avoiding brassica crops. Commonest in damp meadows and moist woods.

DESCRIPTION: The same size as a Small White, though they angle their wings differently in flight and the spring brood males have distinctive pointed forewings. The prominent veins on the underside of the hindwings seldom appear green but are thickly suffused with distinctive grey scales on a yellowy background (see colour section). It can be difficult to separate Green-veined Whites from Small Whites, especially in high summer.

ORANGE TIP (*Anthocharis cardamines*)

Flies during spring throughout lowland, favouring woods, lanes and damp meadows. It breeds primarily on ladies smock and garlic mustard, in a variety of damp and moist habitats. *Anthocharis* means 'grace of a flower' in Greek.

DESCRIPTION: The males are distinctive, with their orange flash on otherwise white wings, but the retiring females become lost among Small and Green-veined Whites. The green marbling on the underside hindwing is distinctive when the female is perched, and the grey forewing tips become prominent once your eye is in (see colour section).

HAIRSTREAKS, COPPERS AND BLUES (*Lycaenidae* family)

We have five species of hairstreak butterflies, seven resident species of blues, two arguses (effectively brown-blues) and one copper. These are pretty and fascinating butterflies.

GREEN HAIRSTREAK (*Callophrys rubi*)

Flies throughout spring in a variety of habitats, breeding on a diversity of food plants. Strong colonies breed on cranberry in lowland peat bogs, on common rockrose on hot downland hillsides, and on gorse on warm heathy slopes. The specific name *rubi* means 'of bramble', on which it sometimes breeds.

DESCRIPTION: Settles only with closed wings. A tiny but distinctive butterfly with emerald-green undersides and deep-brown upper sides. The males are aggressive.

Brown Hairstreak (*Thecla betulae*)

This hairstreak is one of our hardest butterflies to see, occurring only at low population density and being prone to indolence. Flies from late July into early autumn, in woods, meadows and on scrubby downland in landscapes where the food plant, low blackthorn, is common. It is inappropriately named after the Latin for birch, *betula* – it is curious that this erroneous name remains in use when so many other names have been altered. It should be common where blackthorn abounds but most of the over-wintering eggs are destroyed during annual hedge trimming. Best to look for the butterflies early in the morning around ash trees in blackthorn hedges, when the males and females meet up. You will need binoculars. The butterfly obtains sustenance from sticky ash buds but sometimes visits angelica, bramble and hemp agrimony flowers.

DESCRIPTION: Autumnal colours of orange and brown. The undersides are orange with a thin white 'W', and both sexes have distinctive tails, which separates it from the similar-looking common Gatekeeper.

Purple Hairstreak (*Favonius quercus*)

A common butterfly in oak landscapes – *quercus* is Latin for oak – in the lowlands, but it is rarely seen as it is most active on July evenings. Breeds on oaks. Look for grey butterflies performing circle dance courtship flights along sunny sheltered oak edges on still, warm July evenings, especially from 5.30–7.30pm. Take binoculars.

DESCRIPTION: The undersides are grey and the purple iridescence on the upper sides is seen only at certain angles (see colour section).

WHITE-LETTER HAIRSTREAK
(*Satyrium w-album*)

Breeds exclusively on elms, especially wych elm. It favours flowering trees, which are most vulnerable to Dutch elm disease – colonies seldom last long today because of this. Look for the active males chasing each other about high over elms or ash trees near elms, especially in the morning – when two meet, they spiral up together before separating and descending. This flight is diagnostic. Flies during late June and July. Sometimes visit brambles and thistles. Take binoculars to see them properly.

DESCRIPTION: Settles only with closed wings. Smaller than the Black Hairstreak, and lacking black spots on the inner edge of the hindwing orange flash.

BLACK HAIRSTREAK (*Satyrium pruni*)

Breeds on tall old blackthorn. Found only in and around woods in the clay belt between Oxford and Peterborough. Scan the crowns of dense blackthorn thickets with binoculars, looking for battling or exploring males. Visits bramble flowers in hot weather. White-letter and Black Hairstreaks are rarely seen together as blackthorn and elms seldom grow together (the White-letter is also smaller and usually flies later). Black Hairstreaks fly only for three weeks, usually in late June and early July.

DESCRIPTION: Settles only with closed wings. More extensive red markings than the White-letter Hairstreak, with a prominent row of black dots on the inner edge of the orange flash that borders the hindwing underside.

SMALL COPPER (*Lycaena phlaeas*)

A tiny fiery dart of a butterfly that occurs in a variety of habitats, breeding on sorrel leaves in pockets of hot, bare ground. Commonest on heaths, acidic sand dunes and old hay meadows. Occurs in two or three broods, the second of which (in August) is the strongest, from mid-April to late October.

DESCRIPTION: Quite distinctive, being the only British copper-coloured butterfly (see colour section). Basks on bare ground.

SMALL BLUE (*Cupido minimus*)

Flies from mid-May to late June mainly, with a small second brood in early August at its warmest sites. Breeds only in the flower heads of kidney vetch, which grows on downland and sea cliffs. The males can gather in rough grass pockets some distance from the food plant, but usually the butterfly is found near this distinctive plant. Colonies are found in sheltered places. Cupid, was the Roman god of love, after whom we have the genus *Cupido*, though in Latin the word 'cupido' is a noun meaning desire.

DESCRIPTION: Unmistakeable. Our smallest butterfly, minuscule and dusky dark blue. Grey undersides with black dots, without any orange spots.

Silver-studded Blue (*Plebejus argus*)

Breeds mainly on young heathers on southern heaths, where it is locally common. Brighter blue races also occur on limestone grassland around Purbeck in Dorset and the Great Orme in North Wales, where the dwarf race (subspecies *caernensis*) abounds in flowery places on this stunning Carboniferous Limestone promontory around midsummer day, flying alongside a curious small race of the Grayling. Also on sand dunes in west Wales and south-west England. Flies from mid-June to mid-July, usually in dense colonies.

DESCRIPTION: A petite bright blue jewel of a butterfly with lead (rather than silver) studs outside the orange zone on the hindwing undersides. Females are usually brown. Male upper sides have distinctive broad black edges.

Brown Argus (*Aricia agestis*)

Two broods are produced, during May and early June, and again from mid-July to early September. Inhabits downland, calcareous sand dunes and other grasslands, breeding on common rockrose on limestones, but also on tiny cranesbill plants in other dry lowland habitats.

DESCRIPTION: Difficult to identify. A tiny active deep brown butterfly which looks like a small, dark female Common Blue, though the undersides are a brighter grey, the upper-side orange markings are redder and it lacks blue body hairs. The males are territorial and aggressive, which instantly separates them from placid female Common Blues.

NORTHERN BROWN ARGUS (*Aricia artaxerxes*)

The highly similar northern version flies during late June and July on limestone grasslands in Scotland and northern England, breeding almost exclusively on common rockrose, which grows only on limestone.

DESCRIPTION: Smaller orange markings than the Brown Argus and usually features a tiny white mark in the middle of the forewing upper side. Can be confused only with brown female Common Blues, as no other blue butterflies with brown females occur up north.

COMMON BLUE (*Polyommatus icarus*)

Our commonest grassland blue, flying in the south during May and June and again from late July to mid-September. Single brooded, during July, further north. Breeds on birdsfoot trefoils and clovers. Forms loose colonies. Named after Icarus, a pioneer of flight in Greek mythology, who used waxed feathers that melted when he flew too close to the sun.

DESCRIPTION: Males have bright blue upper sides with clear white edges, though these wear away with age. The females are variable – either deep blue or brown – and have orange spots, but always with uninterrupted white margins. These pure white margins, lacking black-vein ends, separate it from the rarer and lovelier Adonis Blue (see left and colour section).

CHALKHILL BLUE (*Polyommatus coridon*)

Chalkhills breed on horseshoe vetch and usually occur in large colonies on limestone hills in southern England, flying from mid-July to late September. There are many wonderful localities and the downs are at their flowery best in mornings in late July and early August, when the short turf shimmers with the sky blue males of the Chalkhill Blues searching for freshly emerged females.

DESCRIPTION: The Cambridge blue of the male makes it easy to identify. It is our lightest blue butterfly (see colour section). The dark brown female is hard to separate from the female Adonis Blue, but Chalkhill Blues are usually old and worn before the fresh females of the second brood of the Adonis emerge. This is the simplest way of separating them. Also, inspect mating pairs closely; this really helps you recognise the females.

ADONIS BLUE (*Polyommatus bellargus*)

Scarcer than the Chalkhill Blue, though breeding on the same food plant, horseshoe vetch, and often occurring in the same locality. Favours shorter turf and is normally restricted to south-facing slopes. Flies in two broods, from mid-May to late June and again during August and September. The latter brood is usually stronger.

DESCRIPTION: The males differ from those of the Common Blue in that they are an electric iridescent blue – if in doubt, it is not an Adonis. The females are dark chocolate brown, though with some iridescent scales near to the body. See also description of Common Blue.

HOLLY BLUE (*Celastrina argiolus*)

The only blue that flits around bushes, and the most common blue butterfly in gardens and parks. Flies in spring and again in July and August. The spring brood lays eggs on the flowers of holly and other shrubs, the summer brood seems to breed exclusively on ivy flowers. Common in some years but more often very scarce, partly due to the weather, with sequences of good springs and summers benefiting the butterfly, but also because its caterpillars are heavily parasitised by the grubs of a tiny black-and-yellow wasp, called *Listrodomus nycthemerus*.

DESCRIPTION: Used to be called the Azure Blue, which befits its colouring. No orange spots on the wing undersides (unlike the Common Blue) – just tiny black spots (see colour section).

LARGE BLUE (*Phengaris arion*)

Declared extinct in 1979 but has since been reintroduced to the West Country using butterflies from Sweden, the Large Blue is now flourishing in the Polden hills in mid-Somerset. The National Trust runs an open-access site for it, Collard Hill near Street (see the National Trust website). Inhabits very hot grassland on south-facing slopes, flying during June. The larvae feed for a while on Wild Thyme flowers before becoming predators of the grubs of a red ant, living underground for 10 months in the ants' nests, from which the butterflies emerge.

DESCRIPTION: Our largest and darkest blue, with no orange on the wing undersides. These features easily separate it from the Common Blue, which is generally between broods when the Large Blue is flying and is smaller and lighter.

METALMARKS
(*Riodinidae* family)

Although a large family globally, only a single species occurs
here in the UK.

DUKE OF BURGUNDY (*Hamearis lucina*)

Flies from mid-April to early June, mainly on rough downland
but formerly in coppiced woods. Found in central southern
and south-east England, the North Yorkshire Moors and the
Morecambe Bay limestone hills. Breeds on cowslip in long
grasses, and occasionally on primrose. Is becoming very rare.
Named after Lucina, the Roman goddess of childbirth and
of the spring.

DESCRIPTION: A tiny fritillary. The upper sides are a
chequer-work of orange and black, the undersides are
browns, orange and silver. The females have three pairs
of legs, the pugnacious males only two.

FRITILLARIES AND ARISTOCRATS
(*Nymphalidae* family)

Eight species of spectacular orange-and-black fritillary
butterflies are resident here. Our seven aristocrats consist
of two admirals, a lady and an emperor, plus the Comma,
Peacock and Small Tortoiseshell.

WHITE ADMIRAL (*Limenitis camilla*)

Our most graceful butterfly in flight, cleverly hugging the foliage contours of trees and bushes. Found in shady woods in southern England, where it breeds on honeysuckle growing in dappled shade. Flies from mid-June to early August. Loves bramble flowers.

DESCRIPTION: Easily identified – our only black butterfly with distinctive white bands. Much smaller and with rounder forewings than the Purple Emperor.

PURPLE EMPEROR (*Apatura iris*)

A giant of a butterfly – brave, bold and fast flying. Very hard to see as it lives above the woodland canopy and occurs only at low population density. Inhabits wooded landscapes in southern England, breeding on shady goat willow bushes. Is on the wing from Midsummer Day to early August. Does not visit flowers but occasionally descends to imbibe from unsavoury substances on the woodland rides, becoming quite approachable. The best of all butterflying experiences – early July in the southern oak woods with the promise of the king of all our butterflies, the Purple Emperor high in the canopy.

DESCRIPTION: You cannot mistake this dark butterfly with white bands: if in any doubt, it is not an emperor! Red and White admirals are much smaller. The male's purple iridescence is seen only at certain angles, whilst the giant females lack the purple and are dark brown.

RED ADMIRAL (*Vanessa atalanta*)

Occurs in all habitats and seen almost year round, often being the first butterfly of the year. Most numerous from early July to late autumn, when it can fly in unusually low temperatures. Breeds on nettle patches. Named after Atalanta, a famous beauty and athlete of Greek mythology, who raced her suitors and killed them if they lost, until one cheated and won her.

DESCRIPTION: The red bands are prominent, making this butterfly highly distinctive (see colour section). There are no other black, red and white butterflies.

PAINTED LADY (*Vanessa cardui*)

Fast-flying when migrating, and the males can be aggressively territorial. Mostly seen from late July through to early autumn but can be seen at any time of year, even on migration in winter. Can occur anywhere. Breeds mainly on thistles – the Latin name *cardui* means 'of thistle'.

DESCRIPTION: Effectively the only pink-looking butterfly, though old, faded specimens look grey (see colour section). Easy to identify when visiting flowers.

SMALL TORTOISESHELL (*Aglais urticae*)

The archetypal garden butterfly, occurring throughout the UK, though it has declined in recent years. The butterflies hibernate, often in outbuildings, before breeding in the spring. A fresh brood emerges from mid-June. This produces a larger brood during August, which feeds upon garden flowers before hibernating. Its gregarious larvae feed within protective silk tents on nettle patches in sunny places.

DESCRIPTION: A distinctive medium-size butterfly with large areas of reddish-orange punctuated by bold black markings, and two prominent yellow patches on the forewing leading edge. The iridescent blue pearls on the outer edges of both wings are distinctive. The undersides are black, grey and buff (see colour section).

PEACOCK (*Aglais io*)

Overwinters as butterflies, which mate and lay eggs in spring. The new brood emerges in July, feeds up for a while then hibernates. Breeds on nettles in sunny places. Common in lowland Britain. Named after Io, who was ravished by Zeus.

DESCRIPTION: Easy to identify, being the only butterfly with huge peacock eyes – RAF markings – on the wing upper sides. The undersides are completely black (see colour section).

COMMA (*Polygonia c-album*)

Found throughout lowland England and Wales, but never seen in any great numbers, being a loner. In spring, the butterflies pair up and lay eggs that produce a lighter-coloured brood from late June; more, darker, butterflies emerge as summer moves into autumn. Breeds mainly on shady nettles, elm trees and hops.

DESCRIPTION: The only British butterfly with jagged but symmetrical wings. Tawny, resembling the autumn leaves among which it often hibernates (see colour section).

SMALL PEARL-BORDERED FRITILLARY
(*Boloria selene*)

Flies a little later in the season than the Pearl-bordered Fritillary, usually from mid-May to late June, and occurs in a wider range of habitats. Found throughout western Britain in sea combes with bracken, heathy commons and hillsides, grasslands on Carboniferous Limestone, some fens and marshes, and woodland clearings, but is in decline. Breeds on violets, particularly common dog-violet and marsh violet.

DESCRIPTION: Hard to separate from Pearl-bordered Fritillary as there is no real difference in wing size. The central zone of the hindwing underside holds four silver splashes punctuated by dark brown splodges with prominent black spots. The female upper sides usually have an obvious pale border, which instantly separates them from the Pearl-bordered Fritillary.

PEARL-BORDERED FRITILLARY
(*Boloria euphrosyne*)

One of our most graceful butterflies in flight, named after Euphrosyne, who was a muse and a grace in Greek mythology. Flies during late April and May over dry woodland clearings, bracken hillsides and scrubby limestone grasslands, breeding on violets growing among dry leaf litter. In severe decline. One of the best butterflying experiences is to see Pearl-bordered Fritillaries on a mid-May morning in the New Forest woods northeast of Brockenhurst. Join this most graceful butterfly as it explores, ceaselessly and frenetically, its beloved woodland rides and clearings.

DESCRIPTION: Much rarer than the Small Pearl-bordered Fritillary, from which it differs mainly by having only two central silver patches on the hindwing undersides, and by lacking dark brown patches with black spots.

HIGH BROWN FRITILLARY (*Argynnis adippe*)

Very rare and rapidly declining, restricted now to a few bracken slopes in the West Country, south Wales and the southern Malvern hills, though it is still numerous locally on the carboniferous limestone hills of Morecambe Bay. Flies from mid-June to late July (late August in northern England). Breeds on violets in warm pockets among dry leaf litter. Visits the flowers of brambles, thistles and knapweeds.

DESCRIPTION: On the wing it is very hard to separate from Dark-green Fritillary with which it regularly flies, but the hindwing undersides have a prominent row of reddish-brown spots with silver pupils, and the forewing outer edge is slightly concave. One of our loveliest, but not a 'beginner's butterfly'.

DARK-GREEN FRITILLARY (*Argynnis aglaja*)

Similar but more widespread than the High Brown, occurring in a greater variety of habitats – downs, cliffs, sea combes and sand dunes, heathy hillsides, bracken commons and some woodland clearings. Found locally throughout the UK, sometimes in numbers. Flies from mid-June to mid-August generally, and tends to occur, somewhat inconveniently, wherever High Brown Fritillaries fly. Breeds on violets among grass tussocks – cooler situations than those favoured by its rarer cousin.

DESCRIPTION: Most females are distinctive, due to the presence of a thick black border on the wing outer margins, framed by buff. The hindwing undersides have silver pearls set among dark green, though that can fade. Males are hard to separate from those of the High Brown (see colour section).

SILVER-WASHED FRITILLARY (*Argynnis paphia*)

The happiness butterfly, big, orange and bouncy – the 'Tigger' of our butterfly fauna. Flies from late June to late August in woodland rides and glades in southern Britain and southern Lakeland. Breeds on violets among tree leaf litter, particularly under oaks.

DESCRIPTION: The males are a rich, bright orange but the females are a duller, fulvous colour (a few females are dark with a green tinge, known as form *valezina*). Differs from other large fritillaries as it has distinctly pointed forewings and there are no silver pearls on the hindwing undersides. The silver is mingled with a green wash (see colour section).

MARSH FRITILLARY (*Euphydryas aurinia*)

Occurs in colonies in marshes throughout western Britain and, curiously, on dry limestone grasslands in central southern England, breeding almost exclusively on devil's bit scabious. Flies from mid-May to late June, in distinct colonies.

DESCRIPTION: Unmistakeable, though somewhat variable. The only fritillary with prominent bands of red on the wing upper sides, which are mixed with black chequered markings and often yellow bands. The undersides are pale red and yellow, and lack silver.

GLANVILLE FRITILLARY (*Melitaea cinxia*)

All but restricted to the Isle of Wight, though it periodically forms colonies on the nearby Hampshire coast and from time to time is released elsewhere by enthusiasts who breed butterflies. Flies during May and June, on the island's eroding under-cliffs and warm chalk downs. Breeds on ribwort plantain growing among sparse vegetation on south-facing slopes.

DESCRIPTION: You should never see this orange and black chequered butterfly flying alongside the similar-looking Heath Fritillary in Britain. But it is much brighter than the Heath Fritillary, and the hindwing undersides lack prominent black markings along the veins.

HEATH FRITILLARY (*Melitaea athalia*)

Restricted to the woods east of Canterbury in Kent, bracken combes on east Exmoor and some woodland clearings on the Cornwall border, though it has also been reintroduced to woods in Essex and Middlesex. Flies from late May to early July. Breeds mainly on common cow-wheat, a curious annual plant that is semi-parasitic on the roots of other plants. One of the best butterflying experiences: seeing Heath Fritillary in profusion in the east Kent sweet-chestnut coppice woodlands. Walk the overhung paths beneath dense, shady chestnut woodland, until you are hit by hot sunlight in a recently coppiced clearing, where this sublime dark fritillary abounds.

DESCRIPTION: Appears much darker in flight than the Glanville Fritillary, especially in the West Country, and is effectively our only black-looking fritillary.

THE BROWNS (*Satyridae* family)

Eleven species of brown butterfly occur in Britain, although one of them is actually black and white. All breed on grasses, usually favouring particular types of grass.

SPECKLED WOOD (*Pararge aegeria*)

Flies from late March (in the far south) to early autumn, and is almost continuously brooded. Usually found in shade close to trees or bushes, and particularly in sun spots along overhung woodland paths. Breeds on soft grasses in dappled shade. Has recently spread to all of lowland Britain.

DESCRIPTION: A medium-size dark butterfly with distinctive pale yellow spots that vary somewhat in size and number (see colour section).

WALL BROWN (*Lasiommata megera*)

Basks, wings open, on dry, bare ground. Was formerly common in England and Wales, but has declined in many southern counties and is now most common along the coast. Two main broods, from early May to early June and late July to early September, with a small and localised third brood during the autumn after hot summers. Breeds on soft grasses on sunny banks and avoids wet places.

DESCRIPTION: The bright orange markings are prominent but not chequered, and the thick black band in the centre forewing of the male's upper side is distinctive. These, and the row of white-centred black spots on the rear margins of the hindwing upper side distinguish it from a small fritillary.

Mountain Ringlet (*Erebia epiphron*)

Identification is not a problem, this being our only mountain butterfly, occurring in diffuse colonies on the central high fells of the Lake District and in the south-west Highlands of Scotland. Most colonies are found above 500m (1,600ft). The only other butterfly flying at that altitude is the Small Heath, which is much smaller and brighter. The flight season is variable, consisting of three or four weeks between early June and the last week of July. It is thought to breed on mat-grass, but colonies are more localised than the plant. The research I conducted in the Lake District found colonies in areas where a layer of sheep's fescue grass occurred among the mat-grass. Perhaps the caterpillars transfer from the finer sheep's fescue to mat-grass as they develop?

DESCRIPTION: Dark brown with orange spots that have a black centre.

Scotch Argus (*Erebia aethiops*)

Identification is easy, as it occurs at lower altitudes than the similar Mountain Ringlet and flies later in the year. An August butterfly, though starting in late July in England, found at Arnside Knott (National Trust) and the old railway line at Smardale east of Tebay. In Cumbria, it flies in dry, scrubby limestone grassland, breeding on blue moor grass at Arnside and a range of coarse grasses at Smardale. It is widespread in the less heavily grazed parts of the hilly regions of Scotland, breeding mainly on purple moor grass.

DESCRIPTION: Black butterfly with red spots. *Aethiops* means dark-coloured.

MARBLED WHITE (*Melanargia galathea*)

Primarily a butterfly of dry limestone grassland in southern England, though it occasionally occurs in dry or damp acidic grassland and has spread as far north as the North Yorkshire Moors. Flies for some five weeks from mid-June through to early August. Prone to flopping lazily around in rough grass and visiting flowers. Breeds on various grasses, particularly where red fescue grows among coarser grasses.

DESCRIPTION: Easy to identify, being the only British black-and-white chequered butterfly (see colour section).

GRAYLING (*Hipparchia semele*)

A seriously cryptic butterfly, which settles on bare ground, wings closed and held at an angle so as not to cast any shadow. This habit helps identify it. Primarily a coastal butterfly, inhabiting sand dunes, cliffs and coastal heaths, though it also occurs on inland heaths and locally on limestone rocks, especially Carboniferous Limestone. Has declined inland, especially on the chalk. Breeds on isolated tussocks of fine-leaved grasses among bare ground. Most colonies fly from mid-July to late August but the dwarf race around the Great Orme in North Wales flies during June.

DESCRIPTION: The upper sides are an attractive meditation in greys and browns. The grey marbled undersides vary from locality to locality, reflecting geology and soil differences. The large black spot in the orange flash on the underside forewing assists identification.

GATEKEEPER (*Pyronia tithonus*)

Flies from early July to late August in dry, bushy places in much of lowland England and Wales, breeding on fine grasses growing in warm shade at the base of bushes. Formerly and appropriately known as the Hedge Brown.

DESCRIPTION: An orange butterfly with thick black borders. Smaller and much brighter than the ubiquitous Meadow Brown. Black twin eyespots with white pupils in the forewing are visible on both sides. The male has a thick black band across the forewing upper side (see colour section).

MEADOW BROWN (*Maniola jurtina*)

One of our most common and most widespread butterflies, occurring in large colonies in all lowland grassland habitats throughout the UK. Flies mainly from early June through to early September, though lingers longer on the southern downs. Breeds on a variety of grasses.

DESCRIPTION: A dark brown butterfly with an orange flash in the forewings, which is larger in the female. Both sexes have a large black spot (visible on both sides), with a single white pupil, within this forewing flash (see colour section).

RINGLET (*Aphantopus hyperantus*)

Occurs in colonies on dry and damp rough grassland in lowland habitats in England, Wales, Scotland and Northern Ireland, favouring woods on clay soils. Breeds on coarser grasses. Flies from mid-June to mid-August.

DESCRIPTION: Looks black when newly emerged, but the colours fade to mid-brown. There are several small but noticeable concentric rings of orange, black and white on the hindwing undersides.

SMALL HEATH (*Coenonympha pamphilus*)

One of our most widespread butterflies, occurring in dry grasslands throughout the UK, up to about 600m (1,968ft). Rare in woods nowadays. Two broods in the south, where it can be seen from early May through to late September, but only a single high-summer brood further north. Breeds on finer grasses, especially fescues. Takes nectar from low flowers such as wild thyme.

DESCRIPTION: Settles only with closed wings. A small butterfly with bright orange upper sides and grey hindwing undersides.

LARGE HEATH (*Coenonympha tullia*)

Restricted to lowland and upland peat bogs in northern England, North Wales, Northern Ireland and Scotland. It is strongly associated with hare's-tail cottongrass, the main food plant. Flies in colonies from mid-June to the end of July, though it is hard to approach and tends to allow itself to be carried away downwind.

DESCRIPTION: Settles only with closed wings. Larger and duller than the small heath, which rarely, if ever, occurs in peat bogs. In Scotland, Large Heath butterflies lack the eye spots on the underside of their hindwings, which are prominent in the races of Wales and northern England.

DAY-FLYING MOTHS

It is often difficult to decide whether an insect is a butterfly or a moth, not least because some moths fly by day. The true, technical difference is in the shape of the antennae, which are clubbed or slightly hooked in butterflies and mainly thin or feathery in moths. Many moths fly only weakly and intermittently by day, usually when disturbed while at rest. But we have some 60 species of larger moth that fly readily in daylight. The following is a selection of the more regularly seen day-flying moths.

BURNET MOTHS (*Zygaena* spp.)

Several types of burnet moths occur in Britain, though some are rare. They fly from early June through to late August in dry grasslands, breeding on birdsfoot trefoil and other vetches. Children often find their straw-coloured cocoons on dead grass stems.

DESCRIPTION: These are strange-shaped moths, with thick black bodies and narrow red-and-black wings (see right and colour section). The most common species are the Five-spot Burnet and the Six-spot Burnet, which have five and six large red spots respectively on their otherwise black forewings, and red hindwings.

CINNABAR (*Tyria jacobaeae*)

Flies from May to August in dry grassy places, including gardens. Settles with wings flat, held in a triangular shape. Breeds on ragworts and groundsels, producing distinctive yellow-and-black striped caterpillars.

DESCRIPTION: A common and unmistakeable red-and-black moth. Note the red bar along the forewing leading edge and the scarlet hindwings.

SCARLET TIGER (*Callimorpha dominula*)

This spectacular moth is rather local, occurring in southern England, though it is increasing at present and can be seen in some towns and cities. On warm late-June evenings they float around in mid-air, and are quite eye-catching. Caterpillars feed mainly on comfrey, growing in damp wasteland and along river banks. The Scarlet Tiger counts as an honorary butterfly.

DESCRIPTION: A distinctive moth with black forewings punctuated by large white-and-yellow spots, and bright scarlet hindwings and abdomens.

HUMMINGBIRD HAWKMOTH
(*Macroglossum stellatarum*)

This migrant moth is aptly named, as it hovers, wings beating frenetically, while sipping nectar from tall flowers. It occurs readily in gardens, visiting buddleias and other nectar-bearing flowers. It is mostly seen in late summer and breeds on bedstraws.

DESCRIPTION: When hovering, the grey-and-orange wings are almost invisible, giving the impression of a large motionless grey bullet, with white side spots (see colour section). Some mistake this moth, especially large females, for genuine hummingbirds, even reporting their sightings to the RSPB!

BURNET COMPANION (*Euclidia glyphica*)

A moth that mimics the Dingy Skipper butterfly in appearance, but crashes moth-like to hide in grass tussocks – unlike the brave Dingy Skipper. Quite common in grasslands during spring and early summer, breeding on various different clovers and vetches.

DESCRIPTION: Like the Dingy Skipper but with distinctive orange flanges on its hindwings.

MOTHER SHIPTON (*Callistege mi*)

Often disturbed while at rest in dry grasslands in spring and early summer. Much larger than a Dingy or Grizzled Skipper, and erratic and unpredictable in flight, unlike a skipper. It breeds on clovers and vetches.

DESCRIPTION: This handsome grey moth has exquisite white wavy lines.

SILVER Y (*Autographa gamma*)

A common grey moth that is very active in daylight and is frequently seen in gardens, hovering brazenly to feed from flowers. A migrant species that often arrives in numbers. Like many common moths it breeds on a wide range of low-growing plants.

DESCRIPTION: The silver 'Y' marking on the forewing is quite distinctive – if you can get close enough to see it.

EGGAR MOTHS (*Lasiocampa* spp.) AND FOX MOTH (*Macrothylacia rubi*)

Something huge and brown or orange careering around at speed, regularly changing direction haphazardly, over heathland and rough grassland is likely to be a male of one of the eggar moths or a Fox Moth – and not a Dark-green Fritillary butterfly, which flies more straightforwardly. There are several species of eggars, some of which are rare. The huge hairy caterpillars feed on low shrubs such as bramble and heathers, and are often found basking along paths.

DESCRIPTION: The commonest is the Oak Eggar, which has deep-brown wings with a yellowy band and a distinctive white spot in the forewing. The Fox Moth is smaller and orange-brown. The males of all these moths have feathery antennae.

GARDENING
FOR BUTTERFLIES

*A huge range of butterflies can occur in gardens,
though much depends on the location. If you are fortunate
enough to live at the foot of a chalk down you may have 30
species of butterfly visiting your garden annually. The vast
majority are just passing through, and you will need to spend
a lot of time in your garden to see them all. The good news is
that there are plenty of things we can do to attract butterflies
into any garden, however small. The two cabbage whites, the
Large White and Small White, will both freely lay eggs on
Nasturtiums in a city window box. I have found their
caterpillars on these familiar, easy-to-grow plants
in a fourth-floor window box!*

GARDEN BUTTERFLIES

There is a range of butterflies that can readily be called garden
butterflies, though their diversity is greater in the warm south
and decreases as you go north. They are mainly bright, large
and showy butterflies that fall into three groups.

First, the big aristocrats, or *Nymphalids* – the Comma,
Painted Lady, Peacock, Red Admiral and Small Tortoiseshell.
In gardens, these magnificent butterflies are most common
during August and September, before seeking to spend
the winter as hibernating butterflies, which then mate
in the spring.

Secondly, the garden whites, including the Orange Tip, which fly in gardens from spring through to early autumn. The Orange Tip is a spring butterfly, flying at the same time as the first brood of the Green-veined White. Both of these tend just to pass through gardens. During July, numbers of the two cabbage whites build up steadily. In spring and again in high summer, Brimstones are on the wing.

Finally, you may see some common grassland butterflies, such as the Speckled Wood, Meadow Brown and, in the south, Gatekeeper and Small Skipper. Here we can also include the Small Copper, Common Blue and Holly Blue. Look out for Holly Blues in April and early May, when the males ceaselessly patrol the sunny edges of bushes and hedges in search of females, especially around holly clumps, and again in late July and August when they fly over ivy patches and visit buddleia flowers. This is the most common blue butterfly in gardens.

GROWING FOOD PLANTS
FOR CATERPILLARS

You may find that you already have a selection of butterfly food plants growing in your garden, from members of the cabbage family (*Cruciferae*) – ornamental and edible species – to plain old garden weeds and grasses.

NETTLE FEEDERS

The caterpillars of the Comma, Peacock, Red Admiral and Small Tortoiseshell all feed on nettles. If you have the space, try to leave the odd clump, especially in sunny situations, such as south-facing banks, where the Peacock and Small Tortoiseshell will lay batches of eggs that produce masses of gregarious larvae. The Peacock is all but restricted to a single brood per year, with its larvae being most prominent in June, but the Small Tortoiseshell has two broods that produce butterflies in high summer and late summer.

The Comma and Red Admiral lay their eggs singly and favour smaller, more shaded patches of nettles, with the Comma often using isolated plants, laying on nettle flowers.

CABBAGE FAMILY FEEDERS

The garden whites, including the Orange Tip, breed on wild and cultivated plants belonging to the huge *Cruciferae* or cabbage family. These plants include honesty, sweet rocket, *Arabis* and even *Aubreitia* – which can all be food plants for the caterpillars of the Large White, Small White and Green-veined White.

COMMON GRASS FEEDERS

You really need to live in the countryside or have a huge old Victorian garden, a paddock or an orchard to see many of these butterflies in your garden. This is because they require areas of old, rough grassland, where their caterpillars feed. They are very particular as to the type of grasses, and the microclimate in which these grasses grow.

The Gatekeeper, for example, breeds on fine grasses growing under the edge of bushes and hedges. The Speckled Wood and Large Skipper breed on isolated

clumps of soft, large-leaved grasses in dappled shade.
The Ringlet breeds on tall, coarse-leaved grasses, while
the caterpillars of the Marbled White start feeding on fine,
narrow-leaved grasses before moving on to coarser varieties
as they grow, and so need a mix of grasses.

The Meadow Brown is more catholic, though it avoids very
rough grassland. The Small Skipper lays eggs on just three
soft-leaved grasses, Yorkshire fog and, more rarely, creeping
soft grass or sweet vernal grass. Its eggs overwinter in the
sheaths of these grasses several centimetres above ground,
and will be wiped out if the grasses are cut during the autumn
or winter. It is very hard to work out a mowing regime that
benefits these butterflies, and doing nothing is scarcely an
option as it encourages tall, coarse grasses. The simplest rule
is probably to cut small areas of your rough grassland on a
mosaic-mowing basis, never cutting more than 20 per cent
of the area at any one time, even in winter.

Many butterflies will benefit if you simply let patches of lawn
grow slightly longer, cutting them on a mosaic basis perhaps
twice a year.

HOLLY AND IVY FEEDERS

The spring brood of the Holly Blue lays eggs on the buds,
flowers and berries of various garden shrubs – notably holly,
but occasionally *Cotoneaster*, privet and *Viburnum* – while the
second brood lays them on the buds, flowers and fruits of ivy.
The caterpillars eat only the flowers and berries.

GROWING NECTAR PLANTS
FOR BUTTERFLIES

The main way in which gardeners can attract butterflies is by growing nectar-rich flowers. There is a huge range of flowering plants that butterflies will visit – annuals, herbaceous perennials, shrubs and trees.

In early spring, butterflies awake out of hibernation and seek nectar from the flowers of crocus and snowdrop, and latterly dandelions. *Aubrietia*, bugle, primulas and sweet rocket are popular in mid to late spring.

During June plants such as hyssop, lavender, red valerian, sweet william and thyme are favoured. The garden really comes into its own during July when buddleia bushes come into bloom, followed by classic herbaceous border perennials such as asters, *Echinops*, *Eupatorium*, marjoram, *Verbena bonariensis* and *Sedum spectabile*, the ice plant.

Finally, ivy blossom is greatly favoured by autumn butterflies, especially the Comma and Red Admiral.

The Comma, Peacock, Red Admiral and Small Tortoiseshell butterflies must build up strength in late summer and autumn to help them overwinter. Nectar-rich autumn flowers, such as Michaelmas daisies and *Sedum spectabile*, are crucial. Commas and Red Admirals also drink juices from rotten fruit in orchards, and get mildly drunk alongside the wasps.

HOW AND WHAT TO PLANT

Bear in mind that butterflies are unlikely to be able to find
a small spray or two of a desirable plant: they are attracted
to huge expanses. Mass planting is the answer. Sunlight and
shelter from wind are also essential – you can easily grow
the right plant in the wrong place, and so fail to attract the
desired butterflies.

It is also worth remembering that the nectar has been
reduced or bred out from many modern cultivars, in an effort
to produce longer flowering periods. This is especially the
case with annuals. The modern varieties of annuals such as
Ageratum and heliotrope scarcely attract any butterflies, or
bees, yet thirty years ago these plants attracted hoards. The
true ice plant, *Sedum spectabile*, has largely disappeared from
garden centres, being replaced by cultivars that are easier
to propagate but hold little nectar. So, seek out the older
varieties, and avoid the now-ubiquitous *Sedum* 'Autumn
Joy', which butterflies and bees scarcely visit.

THE BUTTERFLY BUSH

Not for nothing is the familiar *Buddleia davidii* known as the
'butterfly bush'. It is by some distance the premier plant for
attracting butterflies, moths, bees and hoverflies. Its varieties
come in white, pink, mauve, purple and blue and grow in
any garden soil that is not waterlogged. If you do nothing
more for butterflies in your garden, at least plant a buddleia.

The shrub is named after an early plant collector, Adam
Buddle (1665–1715). There are about 100 species, none

of which is native to the UK, though quite a number are grown in our gardens. Some varieties are more favoured by butterflies than others. At present, the two best butterfly varieties are 'Beijing' and 'Dartmoor'.

'Beijing' is a classic mauve buddleia, somewhat floppy in habit. It flowers quite late in the season, and for a long period, from mid-August into October.

'Dartmoor' bears numerous large sprays of reddish-purple flowers but has a fairly short flowering period, during August. It can overload itself and consequently flop, and really needs to be grown in a well-sheltered corner.

Other common varieties that are good for butterflies include 'Black Knight', 'Lochinch', 'Pink Spread', 'Purple Emperor', 'Royal Red', 'Summer Beauty' and 'White Profusion'.

The other buddleia species that attract butterflies include: *B. alternifolia*, which has silvery leaves and bears long drooping panicles of mauve flowers in early summer; *B. globosa*, which carries rounded clusters of yellow flowers in late spring and early summer; *B. fallowiana*, which has a long flowering period in late summer, producing pale lavender flowers with yellow eyes, and *B.* x *weyeriana*, a hybrid between *B. davidii* and *B. globosa* that produces loose clusters of yellow flowers in late summer and early autumn.

If you grow several buddleias in your garden, prune some early and some late (even in late April) to make them flower over a longer period.

Visit a buddleia bush on a warm, still night, and enjoy the moths too – take a torch.

CABBAGE-PATCH PROBLEMS

Both Small and Large Whites can devastate crops of the cabbage (*Brassica*) family. They are, though, not quite as bad as the Cabbage Moth, whose caterpillars burrow into the heart of cabbages. Here are some options for keeping these pests off.

NET THEM: cover cabbage patches with fine-mesh nylon netting – which will also keep off pestilential pigeons. Crops like sprouts and purple sprouting broccoli should not need netting, as the caterpillars conveniently only eat the leaves, which we ignore.

GROW RED CABBAGE: Cabbage white females seldom lay eggs on these, though unfortunately caterpillars will wander in from infested brassicas.

GROW LARGE PATCHES OF NASTURTIUMS: Cabbage white caterpillars love them. This will not stop them laying on your cabbage crops but you can pick infested leaves off the cabbages and throw them into the nasturtium patch, and enjoy the best of both worlds. Note that a high percentage of cabbage white caterpillars – Large Whites in particular – are parasitised, mainly by small ichnuemon wasps.

THE FUTURE
FOR BUTTERFLIES

*We are only starting to realise how complex and
sophisticated butterflies actually are. Yet at the same
time, paradoxically, they can be remarkably adaptive.
This means that conservationists do not know anything like
enough about what our butterflies truly require, and how
to meet those requirements on nature reserves and in the
wider countryside. The good news is that a vast amount
of vital scientific research is being carried out. We already
know what makes several of our scarcer species tick,
but far less is known about the more common and
more widespread species.*

P ractical conservation knowledge is complex. No two
places where butterflies live are alike, because of local
land-use histories and variations in climate, soils and geology.
So what may work well on one conservation site may not
work on another. Butterflies constantly reinvent themselves,
and conservationists continuously have to rediscover them
in diverse situations.

FRAGMENTATION AND ISOLATION

Over the past 20 years we have discovered that most of
our butterflies, including probably all our rarer ones, need to
exist within clusters of colonies over large areas of relatively
unspoilt countryside. Within these clusters individual colonies
die out from time to time while others spring up. The clusters
need to be loosely connected, so that butterflies can fly easily

from place to place, to colonise and recolonise. That
is – or was – the natural pattern.

If a place where a rare butterfly lives becomes temporarily
unsuitable, as regularly happens, and the colony dies out, then
the chances of it recolonising nowadays are slim. In many
parts of the UK, especially in the lowlands, butterfly sites have
become too fragmented and isolated for the natural processes
of colonisation and recolonisation to function. There is too
much hostile land in the way – urbanisation, motorways and
industrial farming hinder butterfly movement catastrophically.

Of course, we can always try to reintroduce butterflies
artificially, though the success rates to date are surprisingly
low and, crucially, this would be treating the symptoms rather
than the underlying cause. Reintroduction is complex and is
not a panacea for conservation.

The status and distribution of our butterflies is not stable,
and never has been, but is in a continual state of flux. The
problem today is not so much the increasing rate of local
extinction, but the paucity or even complete absence of
new colonisations.

Many wild places – or habitat patches – within a landscape
regularly jump in and out of suitability for a species of
butterfly, due to things like varying rates of vegetative
growth from year to year or fluctuations in the numbers
of cattle, sheep or rabbits – too many or too few. This
even happens on well-managed nature reserves. This is
an important reason why butterflies need to occur within
clusters, or matrixes, of different colonies.

Butterflies are hugely affected by weather. A few days of hot sun can bring them out in numbers, while a couple of days of heavy summer rain can all but wipe out an entire brood. There are good butterfly years and bad ones, with much depending on spring and summer weather. But a summer can also impact on its successor; truly great butterfly years coincide with the second or, ideally, third consecutive good summer. Our butterflies are not unique in this, for many hoverflies, moths and solitary bees are similarly affected, only we are less aware of those insects – and they are nothing like so well recorded.

HOW YOU CAN HELP

If you like butterflies, say so; for if we value butterflies strongly within our culture then society will move to save them. Where there is a will, there is a way.

Join or support the charity Butterfly Conservation. You do not need to be able to identify butterflies, let alone be an expert (and the charity probably has sufficient experts anyway). But it needs more people in its regional branches who are prepared to give time to help out, and who have skills in IT, accountancy, fund-raising, education and, above all, communication. And it needs people who are prepared to stuff envelopes and tap data into computers. It all helps.

Get involved in conservation working parties on your local nature reserve or wildlife site. These places need people who are prepared to chop down and burn up invading bushes, remove rubbish and, above all, talk and mix with visitors, and show groups round and communicate.

Grow butterfly-friendly plants in your garden. Every little helps, for gardens can be vital stepping stones that help butterflies move across difficult urban and suburban landscapes. At the very least grow one or two buddleias, and enjoy the show.

Conservation is essentially an expression of love; science merely helps prioritise and deliver pragmatic results.

THE BUTTERFLY POPULATION MONITORING SCHEME

Butterfly populations at selected locations have been closely monitored since 1976, when the Butterfly Monitoring Scheme was established by the government's nature conservation research wing. The scheme uses data gathered from some 174 sites, spread throughout the UK, using the butterfly-monitoring transect method.

In this, a fixed route is walked each week throughout the butterfly season, in conditions in which butterflies are properly active. Every butterfly that comes within an imaginary box projected in front of the recorder is identified and recorded. It is a precise and constant discipline, which requires good identification skills. The information is fed into a computer database run jointly by Butterfly Conservation and the government's Centre for Ecology and Hydrology (CEH).

The analyses tell us much about how weather and climate affect our butterflies. It is hard to separate the impacts of seasonal weather fluctuations from those of genuine climate change, but more than 30 years of data is certainly showing some clear trends. Most notably, many butterflies are now appearing far earlier in the year than during the 1970s and early 1980s, and several species are regularly fitting in extra broods. Facts like these interest climate-change scientists considerably. You will struggle to find an authority on European butterflies who does not believe, rightly or wrongly, that climate change is an actuality. Our butterflies are shouting loud and clear. They seem to be canaries in the mineshaft.

STATUS AND DISTRIBUTION MONITORING

In addition to the population monitoring scheme, there is a national scheme that records status and distribution, and produces distribution maps. This recording scheme, also run by Butterfly Conservation and CEH, currently includes 7.5 million records, incorporating some from as long ago as 1690. Some 6.3 million are recent, emanating from the recording drive generated by Butterfly Conservation's Millennium Atlas project, which began in 1995. Above all, this shows how successful – and popular – butterfly recording actually is at present.

Scientists are able to analyse both the population data and the distribution data, and determine trends from both sets. Again, this shows how useful butterflies are in helping us understand the dynamics of the environment in which we live. This is, perhaps, the main practical use butterflies have for us today.

Our butterflies are immensely susceptible to change, both beneficial and adverse. Their populations have never been stable, in terms of national status, distribution and size, and never will be. It appears that climate change may impact massively on them, producing a whole new suit of winners and losers over time. Some new species may colonise our isles, of which the most likely would seem to be the Long-tailed Blue, Queen of Spain Fritillary and the continental sub-species of the Swallowtail. Conversely, some of our resident species may be horribly affected by drought, notably the Duke of Burgundy, while northern and upland species such as the Scotch Argus and Mountain Ringlet may retreat further north, and probably uphill. Much depends on the scale and pace of climate change. We will find out, thanks to accurate monitoring processes that were established, crucially, before climate change reared its head.

But land use changes, especially those associated with human population growth and the food and energy needs of the post oil-boom era, may well affect butterflies even more. Yet if we truly value them within our culture, and realise their significance to us, society will provide the resources necessary for us to keep them. They are, after all, as the poet John Masefield so aptly put it, 'the souls of summer hours'.

BUTTERFLY SITES

*Every UK resident species breeds annually on
National Trust land, with the exception of the Chequered
Skipper (Scotland only). The Trust owns an unrivalled
percentage of butterfly-rich sites, in terms of places
supporting an impressive number of species and places
supporting large populations of individual rare species. Many
of the best butterflying in the UK is to be had on Trust land.
Here is a selection of some of the very best. Details on how to
reach these magical places, together with downloadable
maps, can be found on the National Trust website.*

CHALK AND LIMESTONE DOWNLAND

This is overall the UK's richest butterfly habitat. In southern
England, visit Afton, Compton and Brook downs on the
Isle of Wight (blue butterflies, Dark-green and Glanville
Fritillaries, Clouded Yellow); Ballard Down, Dorset (blues,
Dark-green Fritillary, Lulworth Skipper, Clouded Yellow);
Calstone Coombes and Cherhill Down, Wilts (blues);
Cissbury Ring, West Sussex (blues); Collard Hill, Somerset
(Large Blue); Box Hill and Denbies Hillside, Surrey (blues,
Silver-spotted Skipper); Hod Hill, Dorset (Marsh Fritillary);
Ivinghoe Beacon, Bucks (Chalkhill Blue, Duke of Burgundy);
Melbury Beacon, Dorset (blues); Rodborough Common,
Glos (Duke of Burgundy, blues); Watlington Hill, Oxon
(Silver-spotted Skipper).

In northern England, Arnside Knott and Heathwaite,
Cumbria, supports Grayling, High Brown and Pearl-bordered
Fritillaries, Northern Brown Argus and Scotch Argus.

COASTAL HABITATS

Cliff slopes, sea combes and sand dunes support many butterflies. Try Bolt Head, south Devon (Dark-green Fritillary and Silver-studded Blue); Brook and Compton Chines, Isle of Wight (Glanville Fritillary); Holywell dunes, north Cornwall (Silver-studded Blue); Murlough dunes, Co Down (Marsh Fritillary and Real's Wood White); Whitford Burrows, Gower (Grayling and Small Blue).

HEATHS

Most of the National Trust heaths in Surrey support Grayling and Silver-studded Blue. Also, Bramshaw Commons, Hale Purlieu and Ibsley Commons in the New Forest.

MOUNTAINS

Most of the English colonies of Mountain Ringlet are on National Trust land. Try the Fleetwith slopes above Honister Pass youth hostel and Wrynose Breast, above Wrynose Pass.

WOODLAND

Ashclyst Forest, east Devon (Pearl-bordered and Silver-washed Fritillaries, White Admiral); Bookham and Holmwood Commons, Surrey (Purple Emperor, Silver-washed Fritillary, White Admiral); Heddon Valley, north Devon (High Brown Fritillary, on bracken slopes); Mottisfont Woods, Hampshire (Silver-washed Fritillary and White Admiral).

FURTHER READING

There are numerous books that cover the identification of our butterflies, and each year new ones are published. Many of the recent works describe the British butterflies in addition to a selection of northern European species. It is difficult to identify our butterflies from such books, and it may be worth avoiding them unless you travel on the continent.

Asher, Jim; Warren, Martin; Fox, Richard; Harding, Paul; Jeffcoate, Gail; Jeffcoate, Stephen, *The Millennium Atlas of Butterflies in Britain and Ireland* (Oxford University Press, 2001).
An overview of the status and distribution of British butterflies.

Newland, David; Still, Rob; Tomlinson, David and Swash, Andy, *Britain's Butterflies* (WildGuides, 2010, 2nd Edition).
Superb revised identification guide with extensive colour photography including old specimens and eggs, larvae and pupae. An excellent starter guide.

Newland, D.E., *Discover Butterflies in Britain*, (WildGuides, 2006).
A useful guide to places to visit to see British butterflies.

Thomas, Jeremy, *The Butterflies of Britain and Ireland* (British Wildlife Publishing, 2010).
The best book on British butterflies, in terms of accuracy of text and quality of illustration.

Thomas, J.A., *Guide to Butterflies of Britain and Ireland* (Philip's, 2007).
A recommended pocket field guide.

There is a wealth of more specialist books on butterflies, including books on the butterfly faunas of many individual counties. For details of the wonderful history of our engagement with butterflies and moths see the following:

Salmon, Michael, with Marren, Peter and Harley, Basil, *The Aurelian Legacy* (Harley Books, 2000).

Salmon, Michael and Edwards, Peter, *The Aurelian's Fireside Companion* (Paphia Publishing, 2005).

Harmer, A.S., *Variation in British Butterflies* (Paphia Publishing, 2000).
An insight into the world of British butterfly aberrations.

Waring, Paul and Townsend, Martin, *Field Guide to the Moths of Great Britain and Ireland*, 2nd edition (British Wildlife Publishing, 2009).
The best book on British moths and their identification. Includes superb life-size paintings of moths in their natural resting positions.

WEBSITES

There is also much information on websites, though the accuracy of the information can be somewhat variable.

www.butterfly-conservation.org.uk
A dynamic society with active branches in all regions of the UK that welcome beginners.

www.ukbutterflies.co.uk
A superb website specialising in assisting identification and the pastime of photographing butterflies.

INDEX

GLOSSARY

Aberration (or variation): A butterfly with unusual markings.

Breed (on): A verb referring to the species of plant(s) on which the caterpillars of a species feed.

Breeding ground: An area containing suitable food plants on which a particular butterfly species can breed.

Brood: A seasonal hatch of butterflies. Most of our butterflies have one or two broods per year.

Caterpillar (or larva): The second, growing stage of the metamorphosis from egg to butterfly.

Chrysalis: An alternative term for the life stage between caterpillar and butterfly (see pupa).

Cocoon: The silken tent in which the pupa of many moths (but no British butterflies) is formed.

Colony: A loose assembly of butterflies within a distinct place. A cluster of connected colonies can make up an overall population.

Distribution: The extent of territory on which a butterfly occurs in the UK.

Ecology: The branch of biology dealing with how living species relate to each other and their wider environment.

Emerge/emerging: A butterfly coming out of the pupa/chrysalis.

Flight season: The time(s) of year when a particular species of butterfly is flying.

Food plant: Plant species on which caterpillars of a particular butterfly species will feed.

Gregarious: Living closely together. Caterpillars of some butterflies live in large groups, usually within a protective silk web.

Habitat: A place where all the needs of a species are met.

Indigenous: Native to one area.

Larva(e): Technical word for caterpillar(s).

Microclimate: The impact of weather on a small area.

Overwinter: Spend the winter.

Parasite: A small wasp or fly that breeds inside a butterfly's egg, caterpillar or pupa.

Pupa(e): The scientific term for chrysalis.

Sexual dimorphism: Butterfly species in which male and female are differently coloured.

Status: The extent to which a species is common or rare within an area.

Transect method: A scientific method for monitoring butterfly populations in a specific place from year to year.